Managers Learning in Action

Managers Learning in Action takes a wholly original approach to organizational learning. Rather than offering either a purely practical or theoretical context, this text is written by a team of managers and academics, combining theory and practice to create a holistic, and above all realistic, exploration of learning at work.

The managers writing in this text offer real-life examples of management challenges they have met. Whether it is rescuing an ailing organization or managing inter-organizational relations, managing change or managing human resources, many of today's crucial management challenges are addressed. This book covers a range of sectors; the organizations studied here include those in

- high-tech manufacturing
- engineering
- telecommunications
- health care
- transport
- government.

Contributors are drawn from three well-established academic programmes: the Irish Management Institute/University of Dublin Master's in Management Practice; the US Benedictine University PhD in Organization Development; and the Henley Management College DBA. The volume is edited by the academic directors of these programmes.

By offering these managers' own reflections on their experiences in the context of relevant management theory, this text provides an important and innovative contribution both for those studying organizations and for those managers who are currently learning and developing at work.

David Coghlan teaches organization development and action research at the University of Dublin, Trinity College. **Tony Dromgoole** is director of public and degree programmes at the Irish Management Institute and is director of the joint Irish Management Institute/University of Dublin Master's in Management Practice. **Pat Joynt** is professor of management development at Henley Management College and professor of international management at the Bodo Graduate School of Business in northern Norway. **Peter Sorensen** is director of the PhD programme in organization development at Benedictine University, Lisle, IL, USA.

Managers Learning in Action

Management learning, research and education

**Edited by David Coghlan,
Tony Dromgoole, Pat Joynt
and Peter Sorensen**

Routledge
Taylor & Francis Group

LONDON AND NEW YORK

First published 2004
by Routledge
11 New Fetter Lane, London EC4P 4EE

Simultaneously published in the USA and Canada
by Routledge
29 West 35th Street, New York, NY 10001

Routledge is an imprint of the Taylor & Francis Group

© 2004 David Coghlan, Tony Dromgoole, Pat Joynt and Peter Sorensen for
selection and editorial matter; the contributors for their chapters

Typeset in Sabon by
BOOK NOW Ltd
Printed and bound in Great Britain by
TJ International Ltd, Padstow, Cornwall

British Library Cataloguing in Publication Data
A catalogue record for this book is available from the British Library

Library of Congress Cataloging in Publication Data
Managers learning in action/David Coghlan . . . [et al.].
     p. cm.
Includes bibliographical references and index.
   1. Organizational learning. 2. Organizational change. 3. Management.
I. Coghlan, David.
   HD58.82.M3576 2004
   658.4'06–dc22   2003019263

ISBN 0–415–32305–3 (hbk)
ISBN 0–415–32306–1 (pbk)

Contents

Illustrations

Figures

Boxes

Tables

Editors and contributors

The editors

David Coghlan teaches organization development (OD) and action research at the University of Dublin, Trinity College. He has published widely in the area of organization development and action research. His books include *The Dynamics of Organizational Levels* (with N. Rashford in the Addison-Wesley OD series, 1994), *Doing Action Research in your Own Organization* (with T. Brannick, Sage, 2001) and *Changing Healthcare Organisations* (with E. Mc Auliffe, Blackhall, 2003).

Tony Dromgoole is director of public and degree programmes at the Irish Management Institute and is director of the joint Irish Management Institute/University of Dublin Master's in Management Practice, a two-year, part-time, action learning master's for practising senior managers. He is co-editor of *Managing Strategy Implementation* (with P. Flood, S. Carroll and L. Gorman, Blackwell, 2000).

Pat Joynt is professor of management development at Henley Management College and professor of international management at the Bodo Graduate School of Business in northern Norway. His most recent book is *The Global HR Manager: Creating the Seamless Organisation* (edited with B. Morton, Institute of Personnel and Development (IPD), 1999).

Peter Sorensen is director of the PhD programme in organization development at Benedictine University, Lisle, IL, USA. He has published extensively in the field of organization development and appreciative inquiry. He is joint editor of *Appreciative Inquiry: Rethinking Human Organization toward a Positive Theory of Change* (with D. Cooperrider, D. Whitney and T. Yaeger, Stipes, 2000).

The contributors

Akinyinka O. Akinyele is lead executive district manager of a major quasi-governmental organization in the United States, which encompasses

11,000 employees who support operations at four processing plants, fifty-one neighbourhood offices and twenty-seven retail outlets serving 3 million customers. His educational background includes a BA in engineering from the University of Illinois, a master's degree in public administration from Governors State University, and a PhD in organization development from Benedictine University.

Cynthia Deane is a learning and development consultant specializing in strategic management of education and training systems. She has a background in educational management and was chief executive officer (CEO) of a state qualifications agency in Ireland, from 1994 to 2000. She now runs a consulting practice, *Options Consulting*, providing a specialized service to public and private sector organizations.

Christopher J. Ibbott has doctor of business administration and master of technology in systems engineering degrees awarded by Brunel University in the UK, and an advanced postgraduate diploma in management consultancy from Henley Management College. As a chartered engineer, Chris is also a fellow of the Institution of Electrical Engineers, a fellow of the British Computer Society and an accredited mediator with the Centre for Effective Dispute Resolution. He is married with two daughters aged 11 and 9 years of age, is interested in flying, academic business research and regularly (thinks about) attending the gym.

William J. Kohley, PhD received his BSME from Kettering University, MBA from North Central College and PhD in organization development from Benedictine University in Lisle, IL. Bill is vice-president of operations for a private manufacturing company where he has worked since 1985. He continues to publish and present topics on social capital, survey feedback and OD as they relate to executive scholars. He is an active member of ASTD, ODN, Academy of Management and the Organization Development Institute where he serves as marketing director.

Mary Lou Kotecki, a graduate of Benedictine University's PhD programme in organization development, currently manages a worldwide shared services group for a Fortune 500 company. She has presented and consulted widely within the United States and internationally in areas of technological research and engineering, employee development, business performance excellence, action research and organization change. Her most recent publication appeared in the *Organization Development Practitioner* (Fall 2000).

Paddy McDermott is an engineering graduate from National University of Ireland, Galway. He has worked in the health care industry since the early 1980s, holding a number of plant management roles. At the time of writing, he was director of European operations for the company in question and has since taken up a global supply-chain leadership role. His work in this area was part of an MSc programme in management practice at Trinity College Dublin/Irish Management Institute.

Ann Parkinson is now using the findings from her research as well as her experience in an evolving career as Human Resources (HR) consultant and academic, building on her career in HR and organization development. She is also associate faculty at Henley Management College and visiting lecturer at Bristol Business School.

Thomas Schmidt (MSc Mgmt, FCPA, MCILT) has over twenty years' management experience in shipping, in a variety of senior positions. He received the Sir Charles Harvey Award for his thesis 'Managing Rejuvenation in a Mature Business'.

Derek Whelan, since 1993, has been CEO of a medium-sized Irish distribution organization where the majority of shareholders are family members. During the previous eighteen years his experience included a finance directorship in a major overseas construction organization and group controller roles with multinational information technology (IT) and manufacturing organizations. He is the holder of ACCA, CPA and MSc Mgmt qualifications and currently sits on government boards at both chairman and director levels.

Introduction

*David Coghlan, Tony Dromgoole, Pat Joynt
and Peter Sorensen*

Work-based learning or learning-in-action is increasingly recognized as critical to both the survival and development of organizations (Argyris and Schön, 1996; Pedler, 1996; Fisher *et al.*, 2000; Raelin, 2000). Managers utilize their organizational work sites as the locations of learning, not from the distance of a seminar room, but by being immersed in the strategic and operational activities that are structured around their managerial and organizational roles. It is also becoming more common that the academic world of theory and research is appreciating the action and learning of practising managers, particularly by holding postgraduate programmes whereby experienced senior managers bring their organizational actions to exposure to the rigour of action research and action learning (Coghlan and Brannick, 2001). How can the learning-in-action of individual managers contribute, not only to their own learning and that of their organization, but also to our knowledge of organizations and help generate theory about what organizations are really like and how they work? In other words, can managers who learn-in-action be researchers at the same time? This book is an answer to this question. Each of the nine management contributors has successfully completed a postgraduate dissertation on the subject of the study and action in his/her own organization. This book, therefore, aims to address both practice and theory issues in researching and intervening in one's own organization.

Managers are increasingly engaging in action research projects in their own organizations (Bartunek *et al.*, 2000). Issues of organizational concern, such as systems improvement, organizational learning, the management of change and so on are suitable subjects for action research, since (a) they are real events which must be managed in real time, (b) they provide opportunities for both effective action and learning, and (c) they can contribute to the development of theory of what really goes on in organizations.

Contributors are drawn from graduates of three well-established academic programmes which work with experienced practitioners.

The Irish Management Institute (IMI) was founded by a group of business leaders in 1952 as the principal national management training body in

Ireland, and it is formally owned by its business members. By 1975 it had established a strong reputation for high-quality training and executive development programmes. These were seen as supplementing, rather than competing with, the undergraduate and MBA programmes offered by the universities.

In the mid-1970s IMI along with a number of other management development institutes and business schools around Europe was debating the value and effectiveness of executive development programmes being delivered at the time. Were the programmes getting close enough to the manager's job? Was follow-up after the programme end required? Did the learning process need more time than the duration of a typical executive education programme? Could a programme be built around each participant which was individually tailored to help that person acquire the knowledge and skills needed to change him or herself and the immediate working environment? Would this mean less 'knowledge' (in the sense of course content) but greater detail and depth (Mulcahy, 1981)?

IMI was mindful at the time that the participant should have ownership of the learning and should learn how to learn, and also of the trend at the time towards more experience-based courses with less time in class. The importance of a peer group to foster learning by providing opportunities for dialectic was key and the IMI was also mindful of what had been noted in relation to internalized change usually occurring when the issue faced was relevant.

All of these considerations led the IMI to formulate a design for a programme which would attempt to satisfy these requirements. The programme was to be aimed at senior managers with responsibility for achieving strategic change in their organizations. It was felt that real change required a sustained effort over a period of at least eighteen months, so this indicated a relatively long programme. Also, the desired constituency were managers of graduate status who would be attracted by a programme that was seen to be the intellectual level of a master's programme. The IMI found the University of Dublin, Trinity College, to be receptive to the idea. The final design was a two-year, part-time postgraduate degree programme known as the MSc (Mgmt) in management practice, which has been jointly run by IMI and Trinity College since 1975.

The programme design is discussed in greater depth in Chapter 10 by Tony Dromgoole, and four of the chapters in Part I are written by managers who took this programme – Cynthia Deane, Paddy McDermott, Derek Whelan and Thomas Schmidt.

In the United Kingdom, the Henley Management College DBA is designed to enhance global management skills for the twenty-first century. Henley's DBA, first launched in 1992, has participants from around thirty countries worldwide and a strong record of graduations. Close to twenty of the doctors completing the three to five-year programme have used action research in their own organization. The organizations involved vary from the National Health Service (NHS) and the BBC in the United Kingdom to high-tech firms in Asia to medium-sized organizations in Scandinavia. The Henley doctorate programme is one of the largest in the world.

Benedictine University offers two graduate programmes in organization development. The master's programme is the oldest OD programme in the United States, dating back to 1968. The programme has graduated a number of important contributors to the field, including David Cooperrider, the primary originator of the concept and approach of appreciative inquiry. The master's programme has been cited as one of the 'Top Three' OD master's programmes worldwide in a survey of OD scholars and practitioner associated with the OD Institute.

The PhD programme in OD is one of the first PhD programmes in the field and is designed for the working executive and consultant. It is designed to create the scholar-practitioner, and its students, alumni and faculty have received numerous awards based on scholar-practitioner papers and articles from the National Academy of Management (US), the OD Institute and the OD Network. Graduates of the Benedictine University OD and Organization Behavior (OB) programmes hold senior level executive positions in Fortune 500 organizations as well as a number of academic and consulting positions.

Part I, Managers Learning in Action, comprises the stories of the managers' experiences and their learning. The organizations represented in the chapters cover a broad range of organizations – high-tech manufacturing, engineering, telecommunications, health care, transport, and government agencies in the United States, United Kingdom and Ireland. The chapters cover a wide range of subjects. Cynthia Deane explores how she, as CEO of a public sector executive agency facing restructuring because of legislative change, initiated and implemented a learning programme which helped the organization prepare for the future, influence the change process and position itself favourably after the change. Christopher J. Ibbott describes the process of introducing the concept of an *eRelationship* in the context of globalization in the network infrastructure supply chain relationship between a major mobile telecommunications operator (UK) and a supplier in order to leverage cost synergy benefits. Derek Whelan describes how he took over the ailing family business and how he addressed the issues confronting the company. He describes how he took charge of the business as he worked through the phases of the 'taking charge' process of a new manager – taking hold, immersion, reshaping, consolidation and refinement – as he worked through difficult family relationships and changed the nature of the business from a placid and lifestyle nature to a vibrant, growth-oriented and pro-fessional organization.

Ann Parkinson explores the role of the manager as the key to managing the organization's relationship with its employees (the psychological/implicit contract) and their mutual expectations in respect of their careers. It draws on research into employees' expectations, triggered by retention issues, in a high-tech, multinational organization (UK) that had devolved traditional personnel roles to line management. William J. Kohley reflects on the implementation of a two-year 360-degree survey feedback between business units in a mid-size US manufacturing company. The results of both a qualitative and quantitative study are provided to give the reader an assessment methodology for the survey feedback process in their organization. Thomas Schmidt deals with the unique problems that confront managers in mature organizations and seeks to identify an appropriate strategy, structure and culture for a shipping company in such circumstances. It challenges the conventional belief that only a low-cost strategy can offer protection in a mature industry and looks at the nature of maturity itself.

Mary Lou Kotecki recounts how a major health care company chose to contradict industry trends by moving from central to regional customer services. The decision to accomplish this complex change within a very short time period provided significant employee, organizational and customer expectation challenges. It also provided an impetus to seize opportunities and to imagine, to learn and to act on possibilities. Paddy McDermott reflects on his experience as the director of operations for the European region of a multinational and in particular the manner in which change at an international level within the corporation affected development initiatives. He reviews the orientation and alignment of multinational organizations. Akinyinka O. Akinyele explores how his own personal values guide his approach to developing trust with his subordinates and reflects on the impact family upbringing has on espoused values and behaved values in the working environment, the impact organizational culture has on how trust is developed in an organization and how these are operationalized in any organization.

In Part II, Management Learning, Research and Education, as editors each of us has reflected on the managers' experiences and extrapolated to a broader context. Tony Dromgoole explores the theme of action learning, which takes the experience of the job as the starting point and exposes strategic and operational issues as they are experienced in action to a questioning process. He illustrates how an action learning programme can be designed and structured within a postgraduate framework. Peter Sorensen reflects on the manager who engages in a doctoral programme as a scholar-practitioner and discusses how scholar-practitioners, by means of action research, contribute to both the development of knowledge and the application of knowledge to the fields of management and organization development and change. Pat Joynt describes the underlying philosophy of the Henley programme and provides examples of a range of dissertation abstracts. He integrates the research work of the examples through the Eden and Huxham (1996) approach to action research. David Coghlan concludes by discussing the manager as learner and researcher. He explores how the learning process can be taken into research and how the dynamics of insider research play a role in the process.

Intended readership

The profile of the intended reader is the thinking manager, the one who can read the stories in this book and learn from them – rescuing an ailing organization, managing inter-organization relations, managing change, managing human resources and so on. The secondary reader is the academic who may use the book in a course for practising managers and who can integrate the stories with theory. That the contributors are *managers* who are telling the story of their interventions in their organizations and reflecting on the experience in the light of relevant theory provides an important contribution to both understanding organizations and to the development of the learning manager. Each chapter is a stand-alone contribution and so the chapters can be read in any order.

References

Argyris, C. and Schön, D. A. (1996) *Organizational Learning II*. Addison-Wesley, Reading, MA.

Bartunek, J. M., Crosta, T. E., Dame, R. F. and LeLacheur, D. F. (2000) Managers and Project Leaders Conducting their Own Action Research Interventions, in R. T. Golembiewski (ed.) *Handbook of Organizational Consultation*, 2nd edition. Marcel Dekker, New York.

Coghlan, D. and Brannick, T. (2001) *Doing Action Research in your Own Organization*. Sage, London.

Eden, C. and Huxham, C. (1966) Action Research for the Study of Organizations, in S. Clegg, C. Hardy and W. Nord (eds) *Handbook of Organization Studies*. Sage, Beverly Hills, CA.

Fisher, D., Rooke, D. and Torbert, W. R. (2000) *Personal and Organizational Transformations through Action Inquiry*. Edge\Work, Boston, MA.

Mulcahy, N. (1981) Action Learning – the Link between Theory and Practice. Paper presented to the International Federation of Training and Development Officers, Annual World Conference, Dublin.

Pedler, M. (1996) *Action Learning for Managers*. Lemos and Crane, London.

Raelin, J. (2000) *Work-Based Learning: The New Frontier of Management Development*. Prentice Hall, Upper Saddle River, NJ.

Part I

Managers learning in action

Part 1

Managers learning in action

Chapter 1

Learning to change

Cynthia Deane

Context

There is a somewhat clichéd aphorism that says there are three kinds of people: those who *make* things happen, those who *let* things happen, and those who ask, 'What happened?' When an organization is faced with change, some people are content to let it happen, others want to make it happen by managing and influencing it, and some will almost invariably resist or deny it: 'What change? No change!' However, if an organization is about to be abolished and reconstituted with a new set of functions and reporting relationships, as mine was when I undertook the action learning project described in this chapter, there are few options: change must be accepted and managed. Otherwise, the future is a very threatening prospect.

The organization in question (let's call it 'Oldorg') was established in 1991 as an *ad hoc* executive agency of the Department of Education in Ireland. Its role was to set, monitor and certify standards for vocational education and training programmes provided within the public further education sector. In the period from 1991 to 2001, Oldorg developed and implemented a framework for vocational awards, promoted innovation in curriculum and assessment for vocational education and training, and established principles for a national framework of qualifications. In 1999, the government introduced a new legislation which provided for the establishment of a unified national framework of qualifications. Under the Act, Oldorg was replaced by a new agency, 'Neworg', established in 2001, which subsumed the existing functions of Oldorg and considerably extended its remit.

When the legislation was published in 1998, I had been the chief executive of Oldorg for four years. In 1998–2000, I undertook an action learning project as part of the Master's in Management Practice Programme (MPP) run by the Irish Management Institute and the University of Dublin, Trinity College. The project set out to explore how learning could support change in an organization. It involved designing and implementing a learning programme for staff of Oldorg at a time of great uncertainty for the organization, and in a context of vigorous internal and external debate surrounding the introduction of the new legislation. I recognized that it was important for the organization to prepare for the future, so that it could influence the change process and position itself favourably when the legislation was implemented.

When I started the MPP in 1998, Oldorg was a relatively young organization operating in a rapidly changing and expanding environment. There were thirty-five staff, comprising mainly teachers on temporary secondment and civil servants assigned by the Department of Education and Science. Ansoff (1985) proposes a model for assessing the level of turbulence in an organization. Applying this model to the political, economic, social and technological environment of Oldorg in 1998, it was evident that a considerable level of turbulence would arise from changes in policies and structures, in relationships with stakeholders, in markets and products, and in technologies. It was also clear that certain technical, political and cultural changes in the organization would be necessitated by the legislation. In technical terms, there would be new approaches to quality assurance and to validation of learning programmes. Existing systems would have to be adapted to meet the needs of new and more diverse customer groups. On a political level, the new institutional framework would require new coalitions to be formed, with new power structures emerging over time. Underpinning all of this was the cultural dimension of change, which was identified as being of central importance to the implementation of the technical and political aspects. This level of change fits the description of 'upheaval' as defined by Tushman *et al.*, because it involves changes 'of the system . . . not in the system' (Tushman *et al.*, 1991: 17). It is a level of change, in short, for which Oldorg was not yet ready.

Having identified what needed to change, the key question was how to implement the change. Posing the question in a slightly different way: could people learn to change? Before seeking an answer, it is helpful initially to consider the nature of the change process itself. A simple model of change comprises three distinct elements: a vision of the future, an analysis of the present, and management of the transition from 'here' to 'there' (Beckhard and Harris, 1987). Applying this model to the situation in Oldorg, it was clear that the first two stages of the process had been completed. A vision of the future had been formulated, by examining the given and the possible dimensions of the change arising from the legislation. There had also been an analysis of the present state and an identification of key change issues, focusing in particular on the cultural aspects. What was needed was to complete the process by managing the transition to the changed state. This called for a high level of openness to change across the whole organization. In effect, it called for a dynamic and continuous learning process at both individual and organizational level, to cope with the rate of change in the external environment. While in the past Oldorg had worked through change by learning in a largely intuitive and informal way, I now proposed to adopt a more systematic approach. This would closely link the themes of learning and change, first, to effect change through learning, and second, to discover how change could act as a catalyst for learning.

Emergent issues for action

As chief executive I recognized that it was my responsibility to prepare the organization for the future, to predict and plan for change, to influence the change process, and to protect and preserve what was important to the organization in the new situation. I was aware that this presented a great challenge to my leadership: a great deal depended on managing the process effectively, both within and outside the organization. I approached the action learning project with three main questions: *Why* do we need to change? *What* needs to change? *How* can we change? In the early part of the MPP programme, there was an opportunity to examine the organization from a number of perspectives: culture, structure, strategy and environment. This analysis was very helpful in clarifying why change was needed. It was also interesting to discover that a small non-commercial public-sector service organization such as Oldorg had much in common with larger private-sector companies, and even with multinational corporations encountered either in the literature or in case histories presented by class colleagues. The areas of commonality mostly centred around *people* issues, and on the importance of addressing these issues in any change management programme.

Having identified the major reasons why change was necessary, I moved towards answering the second question: *What* needs to change? To the casual observer, it might seem that the change envisaged in the legislation was cosmetic, a mere name-change. 'All that is needed is to change the name-plate on the door and the stationery' was the view expressed by a colleague from another organization affected by the legislation. However, a closer examination of the legislation indicated that it would mean that the new organizations would have to develop new relationships with stakeholders, serve new customers, adopt new processes and new technologies, and provide new products and services to a bigger market. This was a level of change that could not be taken lightly. The technical and more particularly the political and cultural aspects needed to be recognized and addressed.

One of the concepts that I found particularly helpful in the change management literature was the idea of a 'constellation' of change issues, with a complex set of interrelationships between them. Allied to the notion that it is almost impossible to change only one thing, this concept helped me to frame a change agenda for Oldorg. Focusing mainly on the cultural aspects of change, for which it was suggested by the earlier analysis that the organization's readiness was low, the action learning project then sought an answer to the final question: *How* can we change? Before I started the Management Practice Programme, I had become aware that 'learning' was increasingly being cited as an instrument of social and organizational renewal. Phrases such as 'the learning society', 'lifelong learning', 'the learning organization', 'organizational learning' and 'action learning' were commonly used in contexts as diverse as management practice and community development. It seemed that a learning approach might provide an answer to the question of how to change. I had a suspicion, however, that what I knew as learning from my career background in education and training was not the same as these new concepts of learning. I thought that there might be an opportunity in the course of the MPP to achieve synergy between my known world and the less well-known area of management practice.

Because my organization was in the 'learning business', it seemed interesting to explore a range of theoretical and practical approaches to learning in organizations, in an attempt to identify a set of principles for the project. I thought that this might also afford an opportunity for the project to make a more public contribution in terms of supporting learning in other organizations. The search for synergy was addressed by reviewing current curriculum and assessment theories and practices to establish whether they could make any contribution to the thinking on learning in organizations, and vice versa. It was rewarding to find that there were considerable points of linkage and complementarity, and this provided a good starting point for the action part of the project: using a learning approach to prepare the organization for change.

Throughout the action learning project, I was conscious of my own role as a change agent and mindful of the fact that there were certain skills required of that role. These mainly centred on setting goals and priorities within the change agenda, and getting others to buy in, through communication, negotiation and managing key relationships. I was also aware that there were certain skills gaps that I had to address through my own learning. I needed to achieve a balance between controlling and enabling the change process. I had to learn to be more comfortable with ambiguity and uncertainty. There was a constant awareness that fear of the unknown produces emotional and political tensions in an organization, so I needed to be watchful to prevent this becoming destructive. Throughout the whole process, there was a risk that the organization, or individuals, would suffer from overload because of the stress of managing both continuity *and* change. The support of the MPP programme itself proved invaluable in this regard.

The action learning project might be visualized as starting with the broad examination of the organization in its environment, then proceeding to an analysis of change issues and to the design and implementation of an intervention to manage the change. At the end, there was an opportunity to reflect on the various layers of learning that had happened: 'for me' – my own personal growth through this learning process; 'for us' – the effect of the intervention on the organization; 'for them' – the possible relevance of the project to other organizations.

Telling the story

The concept of organizational learning and its implementation in the form of the learning organization have become widespread since the late 1980s. A varied literature has emerged on the topic, and many writers have tried to describe the concept and characteristics of a learning organization. Some of the classical literature in the area suggests that a learning organization:

- continually expands its capacity to create its future (Senge, 1990);
- facilitates the learning of all its members and continuously transforms itself (Pedler *et al.*, 1992);
- encourages double-loop learning, whereby not only is an immediate problem or concern addressed, but also the deeper organizational structures are changed for the better (Argyris, 1990);
- responds to changes in its internal and external environments by detecting and correcting errors in organizational theory-in-use and embedding the results of that inquiry in private images and shared maps of organization (Argyris and Schön, 1996);
- learns from mistakes, seeing learning not as a confession of ignorance, but as the only way to live (Handy, 1992).

These multiple perspectives suggest that there is no single, or simple, way to define 'the learning organization'. While it is clear that learning is seen as a 'good thing', not only for individuals, but also for organizations and for society, it is not clear how best to ensure that learning happens in an organization, and how effectively learning can support change. The literature needs to be interrogated for answers to two key questions. Can people learn to change? What learning approaches can best support the changes needed in a specific organizational context?

Having considered the two major branches of organizational learning and the learning organization, each was found to have some merit, while at the same time neither offered a totally satisfactory framework for the purpose of the Oldorg project. A range of action-based strategies was also explored, and this produced many useful insights into effective ways of making learning happen in organizations. Finally, some consideration was given to the possible contribution that curriculum theory and practice could make to the design of a learning programme for an organization. This equally offered helpful guidance, arising from a perceived congruence of thinking on many key learning issues. While no single model of theory or practice emerged as suitable for adoption in its entirety, it was nevertheless clear that an effective learning programme could be designed and implemented incorporating the best elements of the approaches considered. One of the major concepts emerging from the literature was a view of learning as a cultural, as well as a cognitive, construct (Cook and Yanow, 1996). This perspective helped to integrate the conceptual, action and practice-based approaches to learning within the learning programme.

Guidelines for a learning programme in an organization

It was possible to discern from the literature some of the key features of good practice and critical success factors in implementing a learning approach in an organization. The following guidelines adopted for the design and implementation of a learning approach to support the change process in Oldorg were drawn from the literature reviewed, and they incorporate both principles and practical guidance for action:

1 Learning can help people see their current reality more clearly.
2 Highlighting the difference between vision and current reality can generate a creative tension, which leads to successful learning.
3 The shared vision of a group leads to creativity and innovation.
4 Team learning happens through processes of dialogue and discussion.
5 The management and inclusion of diversity is crucial to learning in organizations.
6 Organizational learning can occur when individuals within an organization experience a problem and inquire into it on the organization's behalf.
7 An effective learning system in an organization needs effective channels of communication; information systems; a conducive environment; appropriate procedures and routines; systems of incentives; flexible and co-operative patterns of interaction.
8 Organizational learning can be achieved only by a group.
9 Learning can be tacit: it does not need to be explicit.
10 Learning does not always involve correcting errors: it can also focus on preserving what is 'right'.
11 Knowledge, and therefore learning, is best produced in service of, and in the midst of, action.
12 Action learning can be a first step towards linking individual learning with systematic learning and change in an organization.
13 People in organizations can be helped to reflect on and improve their practices by examining the conflict between their values and their practice.
14 Effective learning is democratic, participative, emancipating and experiential.
15 A good learning programme is holistic, integrating cognitive, cultural and behavioural dimensions; directed by the learner; focused on process as well as product; designed to encompass a diversity of learners and learning contexts.

Implementing a learning programme

Based on the principles outlined above, a learning programme was designed and implemented between September 1998 and June 2000. Simply stated, the purpose of the programme was to ensure that all staff members were given the opportunity to participate in focused learning activities to help them prepare for the changes ahead. The methodology was based on the guidelines emerging from the review of the literature, and built on existing practice in the organization. The technical, political and cultural change issues identified by the earlier analysis dictated the content of the programme. A list of the desired outcomes under each of these headings is given in Box 1.1.

The programme comprised a number of learning modes, targeted at producing specific learning outcomes for individuals and for the organization asa whole. The programme is outlined in Box 1.2, which shows for each

Political

- Influence key decision makers on implementation of legislation;
- Form alliances with key organizations in preparation for post-legislative situation;
- Ensure acceptance of proposed changes among major interest groups, e.g. staff unions, teacher unions, educational management bodies;
- Influence development of national qualifications policy;
- Maintain position of Oldorg as key player in post-legislative situation: link with interdepartmental implementation group, consultancy study;
- Negotiate staffing and career structures for new organization.

Technical

- Change candidate data systems – electronic entries;
- Make systems more flexible and inclusive – work-based learning;
- Make module descriptor more transparent – review;
- Streamline assessment procedures – review;
- Develop and evaluate models for supporting customers (course providers);
- Develop new partnership model of national certification with other bodies;
- Examine technical aspects of legislation;
- Compile information for consultancy study on post-legislative structures.

Continued

Cultural

- Enhance quality assurance focus;
- Improve customer orientation;
- Explore ways of rewarding performance;
- Communicate change issues to staff of organization;
- Promote 'buy in' to change;
- Clarify goals and vision of organization in preparation for transition;
- Deal with resistance, uncertainty, ambiguity of transition state;
- Build readiness and capability for change through continuous learning.

Box 1.1 Desired political, technical and cultural outcomes.

element: the participant group; the learning principles incorporated; the change focus, and the period within which it took place. As can be seen from this outline, the learning programme was both extensive and intensive over the period of the project.

Programme element	Participant focus	Principles incorporated	Change focus	Time
Learning audit	All staff	• Assess state of learning	• Technical • Political • Cultural	Feb. 2000
Project/ task teams	All develop-ment staff. Relevant administrative staff	• Shared vision • Team learning • Including diversity	• Technical • Cultural	Sept. 1999–June 2000
Action learning group	Open to all staff	• Examining values/practice • Inquiring into a concern • Linking individual/ organizational learning • Directed by learners	• Technical • Cultural	Nov. 1998–April 1999 Nov. 1999–April 2000
Staff seminars	All staff	• Shared vision • Dialogue and discussion • Diversity • Channels of communication • Co-operative interaction	• Cultural • Technical	Various dates 1999–2000

Continued

Programme element	Participant focus	Principles incorporated	Change focus	Time
Away days	All staff	• Shared vision • Team learning • Conducive environment • Flexible interaction • Preserve what is 'right' • Democratic participation	• Cultural	June 1999 June 2000
Future focus group	Representative group of ten staff members	• Future visioning • Creativity and innovation • Diversity of perspectives • Group learning	• Political • Cultural	April–June 2000
Training	Open to all staff. Individual/group participation	• Based on needs of individual/organization	• Technical	1999–2000

Box 1.2 Outline of learning programme.

Reflection: reviewing the learning programme

The key question at this point is whether the intervention made any difference. In other words, was the organization any better prepared for change because of having approached learning in a systematic and structured way over the period of the learning programme? The aim of the programme was to convert management vision and commitment into action, to embed a learning culture into every part of the organization by supporting and enhancing the learning of all individuals and thereby of the organization as a whole. As described earlier, there was a great deal of change happening over a short period of time. The contribution of the learning programme to the successful management of the transition state needs to be examined more closely. It is particularly useful to consider the effects of the programme on the cultural, technical and political aspects of change, and especially to check whether the desired outcomes under each of these headings, as outlined in Box 1.2 have been achieved.

Cultural aspects

Among the cultural outcomes that were identified as desirable at the outset of the project were dealing with resistance, uncertainty and ambiguity; promoting 'buy in' to change among staff; clarifying future vision; building readiness and capability for change in the organization. The learning programme included whole-staff events both on and off-site, targeted training inputs and project teams. All of these contributed to a climate of openness to change and an ownership of the process. It is clear that open communication and sharing of information with all staff helped allay fears and resistance, while at the same time enabling people to take responsibility for aspects of the change process. There was a sense of confidence and optimism that 'we can handle this'. This was enhanced by the empowerment of project teams to develop solutions for the future by examining the new legislation and reviewing existing practice. As a result, there was a high level of 'buy in', and resistance and uncertainty were minimized, if not entirely eliminated.

Political aspects

As shown earlier, the change in the organization had a strong political dimension. Since the legislation was published in the spring of 1999, there had been a growing awareness within the organization of the political aspects of the change ahead, engaging both the board and the staff in considering the implications for the future. The position taken by us was not to wait passively for change to happen, but to act positively to influence and shape the change. During the period of the project, there was much political activity, involving contact with external agencies, mostly by the chair of the board and the CEO. There was a danger that members of staff could feel isolated from these discussions and even suspicious or distrustful of what might be decided without their involvement. This was not the case, however, because there was a commitment to open communication within, and participation by, the whole organization in formulating our position in the discussions.

A significant event in the political process was the appointment of a consultant in May 2000 to report to the government interdepartmental implementation group on the staffing and management structures for the new organizations to be established under the legislation. This was seen by the board and staff as a key opportunity to influence the shape of things to come. The future focus group formulated a submission in response to questions posed by the consultant. The group then prepared another document examining the Neworg functions and analysing the changes needed in the organization to perform these new functions. This was an extremely valuable exercise for the organization, and the learning programme had a direct impact on the way it was handled. First, staff members, having had opportunities to engage in collective visioning and other future-focused activities, were fully aware of the possibilities presented by change. Second, the learning undertaken by individuals and groups had enhanced their capacity to communicate, to negotiate and to handle the challenges of change.

Technical aspects

The learning approach adopted had considerable impact on preparing the organization for the technical aspects of change. All staff had been encouraged to enhance their skill levels through training and to work with cross-functional teams for a number of years. There was a movement away from rigid traditional hierarchies and an emphasis on collaborative working. This required people to engage in learning new skills and new ways of working. They were supported in this by the provision of formal training, both on and off the job. However, the 'training' model was not considered entirely adequate in many respects. The learning programme grew from an awareness of the many inadequacies of training. That is not to say that training was completely rejected, a course of action that would be both unwise and impossible in an environment of complex change. What emerged was a diverse learning approach, comprising action learning, training, and group/team activities and whole-staff events.

A number of project teams worked on technical aspects of our systems in preparation for the post-legislative organization. These projects focused on assessment systems, candidate entry systems, work-based learning, accrediting prior learning, quality assurance and communications. In the period from September 1999 to June 2000, significant progress was made in relation to the desired technical outcomes listed in Box 1.1. Candidate data systems were modified, assessment procedures were streamlined for all modules, and the module descriptor was revised to make it more transparent to learners and assessors. The learning programme influenced the working method of the project teams and progress was enhanced by the sense of empowerment that developed among the teams.

Reflections on personal learning

When I arrived at a point where the action learning project was finished, or rather where the action is completed but the learning was continuing, the challenge was to determine what contribution the project had made to the three areas of knowing: *for me*, *for us* and *for them*. In the view of Reason and Marshall (1987), research *for them* produces generalizable ideas and outcomes that elicit the response, 'That's interesting'. To the extent that research is relevant to their practice, research *for us* produces the response 'That works' from people struggling with problems in their own field of action. Research *for me* responds directly, both in process and outcomes, to the individual's 'being-in-the-world', and so elicits the response, 'That's exciting'. It is worthwhile to reflect more deeply on each of these areas in relation to this project, while also recognizing that they are to a large extent interdependent.

For me: 'That's exciting'

For me, the MPP has been without doubt the most valuable learning opportunity of my professional life. I was CEO of the organization for four years before I started the programme. I had spent about half of my previous working life in senior management positions in education without having had any formal management training. Much of my approach to management, apart from what I had gleaned from short courses or personal study, was intuitive and based on my professional training as a teacher. By 1998, however, I had become aware that instinct and intuition had their shortcomings and I felt the need to invest something in my own professional development, especially in the context of imminent change in my organization. I shopped around for a programme that would suit my circumstances and my approach to learning. In choosing the MPP, I trusted my intuition and I feel that my choice was richly rewarded in the benefits I gained from the programme.

On the 'hard' side, to use a crude distinction, the action learning programme gave me a greater awareness of the relevance of general management theory and practice to a public service organization. It also gave me an understanding of the range of management issues faced in common by all organizations. I developed confidence in applying theoretical models of change and strategy development to my own organizational practice, thereby getting to know my organization in a new way. It was also very satisfying to discover that the known world of education and the great unknown of management and learning in organizations offered many opportunities for synergy.

It is perhaps on the so-called 'soft' aspects that there was the greatest growth, however. The MPP provided a unique 'space' where personal growth and learning can happen. At times I felt challenged, unsettled, invigorated and exhausted by the work of the programme. But at all times I was affirmed as a learner and as a person, and was able to reclaim some personal qualities with which I had come to feel very uncomfortable over many years. This applies especially to leadership skills, which I had come to see as 'bossiness' but now can value more highly. I moved through the cycle of 'taking in', 'making sense' and 'taking action', developing the capacity to see issues in a new way and to feel more comfortable with uncertainty and ambiguity, both in myself and in others. This was a very significant and deeply affecting outcome of the programme for me.

I consider myself fortunate to have been a member of my MPP group. As a group of management professionals, they represented a wide range of organizations and a high level of expertise in their specialist areas. Their knowledge instructed me and their experience greatly broadened my horizons. As a group of co-learners, they were warm and generous in their support of each other. They were quite simply the most 'exciting' part of the programme. The fact that the structure of the MPP makes it possible for such close interaction and bonding to develop between participants is a key strength of the programme. It is a good learning model, and one that I would try to replicate in any further work I do in this area.

For us: 'That works'

The period during which I undertook the action learning project was one of great uncertainty as outlined above. The organization had already had seven years of *ad hoc* existence and several 'false starts' when it appeared that it might become statutory. During all of this period, the organization was to some extent working on borrowed time. The term of office of the board was extended twice. Staff secondment contracts were renewed from year to year, with the hope that each year would be the last of the temporary arrangements. Following the passing of legislation, there was a long delay before an interdepartmental implementation group was established to recommend a process for enacting the provisions of the Act, including the establishment of Neworg, the new body to replace Oldorg. In the mean time, there was a change of government minister and a further delay before a consultant was appointed to advise on establishing the new bodies. All of this contributed to a sense of uncertainty at board, staff and customer levels. Each group had its own concerns: political status, jobs, continuity of service provision. As chief executive, my main concern was with keeping the organization running effectively in an environment of strong growth and considerable uncertainty about the future. My aim was to reassure staff that the future of the organization was safe, even if the legislation meant great change. Oldorg would cease to exist in its current form, but its work would grow and continue under Neworg. I held the view that the best way to prepare for change was to own it: shape it, influence it, manage it, and embrace it in every possible way. I played an active part in the drafting of the legislation, so it was no surprise when it was published that the language was very much Oldorg language. I also maintained very good working relationships with all key stakeholders throughout the past few years, recognizing that forming the right coalitions was an important strategic objective at this time.

Inside the organization, there was always an enthusiasm and sense of mission among staff: the classic young entrepreneurial organization, in many ways. People were encouraged to gain new skills and everybody on the staff participated in some formal learning activity, either on or off the job, in the period 1998–2000. It is clear to me that adopting a systematic approach to learning over two years helped the organization to build its readiness and capability for change in many important ways. New technical processes were introduced to help deal with the growing volume and diversity of learners seeking certification. A new political awareness had grown, and with it the capability to influence the change process. Mostly, however, learning changed the culture of the organization.

Schein (1996) maintains that one of the main reasons that organizations fail to 'learn how to learn' is that they are made up of three subcultures, each with its own assumptions: the internal operator culture, the engineering culture made up of those who drive the core technologies of the organization, and the executive culture, including the CEO and senior management. He argues that instead of trying to achieve organizational learning, it is better to create communication between these groups by encouraging cross-cultural dialogues, and also to help learning communities from each of the cultures learn in ways that are appropriate to them. I would maintain that the organization, through the intervention implemented as part of this action learning project, became an effective community of learners, providing a range of learning modes to suit all three cultures and all individuals. This helped manage the transition state to date, particularly in reducing resistance and uncertainty. My view of the learning programme as having been successful in preparing the organization for change was strongly affirmed by feedback, both formal and informal, from colleagues.

For them: 'That's interesting'

What is likely to be interesting to other organizations, other managers, about what happened? A number of aspects of the project might be suggested. For example, the discovery that much current mainstream management theory and practice was extremely relevant to a small public-sector service organization came as somewhat of a surprise to me. It would probably also surprise others in similar organizations, who sometimes dismiss much management thinking as 'not for us'. This, it must be admitted, is said mainly from a position of ignorance. Moving to the more substantive work of the current project, two major aspects might have relevance *for them*: process and product. From the point of view of process, other organizations and managers might be interested to hear that people can *learn to change*, that learning in a planned and systematic way can support and enable change in an organization. They might be sufficiently interested to consider trying to incorporate some of the practices and key principles of the learning programme into a learning programme for their own organization.

In product terms, perhaps the major outcome of the project *for them* is the action research module. This enables learners to gain credit for action research undertaken in a work context or elsewhere. The module offers an opportunity for people at any level in an organization to participate, either individually or in groups, in learning programmes designed around an action learning model. The module does not specify the context or methodology of the programme, so there is complete flexibility for this to be designed to meet the needs of learners. Assessment is through a project and a learner record, and this is consistent with an action-based learning approach. The module is available for certification within the new national qualifications. This means that those learners in organizations who aspire to having their learning formally accredited can now do so within a recognized national system.

I gave this chapter the title 'Learning to change'. I now see that to learn is to change: once one has learned something new, one is inevitably changed. I am changed, having experienced in Séamus Heaney's words,

> The dazzle of the impossible suddenly blazed across the threshold,
> A sun-glare to put out the small hearths of constancy
>
> ('Station Island, X', 1984)

The 'impossible' no longer looks impossible, and the 'small hearths of constancy' are maintained precisely because they are 'constant'. Learning to encompass this duality has been for me the key experience of the MPP.

References

Ansoff, I. H. (1985) Strategic Response in a Turbulent Environment, in W. Guth (ed.) *Handbook of Business Strategy*. Warren, Gorham and Lamont, New York.

Argyris, C. (1990) *Overcoming Organizational Defences: Facilitating Organizational Learning*. Allyn and Bacon, Boston, MA.

Argyris, C. and Schön, D. A. (1996) *Organizational Learning II*. Addison-Wesley, Reading, MA.

Beckhard, R. and Harris, R. T. (1987) *Organizational Transitions: Managing Complex Change*. Addison-Wesley, Reading, MA.

Cook, S. and Yanow, D. (1996) Culture and Organizational Learning, in M. Cohen and L. Sproull (eds) *Organizational Learning*. Sage, Thousand Oaks, CA.

Handy, C. (1992) *Managing the Dream: The Learning Organisation*. Gemini Consulting, London.

Pedler, M., Burgoyne, J. and Boydell, T. (1992) *The Learning Company*. McGraw-Hill, Maidenhead.

Reason, P. and Marshall, J. (1987) Research as Personal Process, in D. Boud and V. Griffin (eds) *Appreciating Adult Learning*. Kogan Page, London.

Schein, E. H. (1996) Three Cultures of Management: The Key to Organisational Learning in the 21st Century, *Sloan Management Review*, 37(3): 9–20.

Senge, P. (1990) *The Fifth Discipline: The Art and Practice of the Learning Organization*. Doubleday, New York.

Tushman, M., Newman, W. and Romanelli, E. (1991) Convergence and Upheaval: Managing the Unsteady Pace of Organizational Evolution, in H. Mintzberg and B. J. Quinn (eds) *The Strategy Process: Context, Concepts and Cases*. Prentice Hall, Englewood Cliffs, NJ.

Chapter 2

Interorganizational relationship transformation in a global virtual community

Christopher J. Ibbott

Context

This study concerned the global transformation in the supply chain of the relationship between two global organizations in the mobile telecommunication industry. Specifically, the customer organization comprises a portfolio of equity interests in a multiple of mobile network operators, and the supplier is a manufacturer of cellular network infrastructure whose relationship with the customer organization was vested in multiple local or in-country pre-existing relationships globally. While the two organizations have their own separate history, they have a business relationship that dates back to 1985.

The customer is the largest mobile network operator in the world, with 112.5 million proportionate customers (as at 31 December 2002) across twenty-eight countries through either wholly owned subsidiary operations, majority owned firms or affiliates. It is the first or second operator in twenty-four of the countries, and has approximately 25 per cent of the global customer base. Based in Newbury, England, the customer has risen since its inception in 1982 to become one of the largest UK firms by equity value, and on the same basis is one of the ten largest companies in the world. The Swedish supplier operates in more than 140 countries, providing both cellular network infrastructure and terminals (handsets) – now through a joint venture – to mobile network operators. The supplier is the world's largest supplier of network infrastructure and the customer is its largest global infrastructure customer.

In 1998, in response to a customer objective to achieve supply cost synergies across its equity interests in mobile network operators, I agreed with the supplier to harmonize globally their in-country buyer–seller relationships; see Figure 2.1 for the diagrammatic details of the initial interorganizational relationships (p. 29). The acquisition of cellular network infrastructure represents a significant proportion of the customer capital expenditure, with a supply chain characterized as the acquisition of high value capital goods and high vendor switching costs. This globalization initiative was and remains a unique and leading initiative for the tele-communications industry that is a process-oriented journey paradigm, through which progress was perceived and guided in an experiential process executed as situated change; meaning one that can accommodate the unexpected dynamically and yet remain focused on the realization of the objective (Orlikowski and Hofman, 1997: 11) or 'an ongoing improvisation enacted by organizational actors trying to make sense of and act coherently in the world' (Orlikowski, 1996: 65). This experience may be seen as a journey that not only mobilized a transformation towards globalization, but also generated knowledge about future such opportunities and how they should be managed. As improvisational change this transformation did not follow a project plan, however the customer did have (and continues to have) a financial objective, an agreement with the supplier to proceed with a strategy of globalization absent of any conscious definition of exactly what that meant, no dedicated team, no definitions of responsibilities and account-abilities, and the effort was not budgeted; a somewhat counterintuitive approach to the norm. Nevertheless, network operators and the supplier both provided (and continue to provide) resources at the expense of their oper-ations to participate in and make successful this transformational endeavour.

The longitudinal period of transition of this study ran approximately from January 1999 through to September 2000, whereupon a number of the mutually identified integration streams had been implemented, piloted or committed to operationalization. During this period major changes were also afoot in that the customer completed a merger (30 June 1999) and a subsequent acquisition (sanctioned by the EU Commission 12 April 2000) through which the mobile operator interests of the customer were expanded, certain of which later joined this globalization endeavour with the supplier. The acquisition proposal included a public commitment to the financial markets of a range of synergies, cellular network infrastructure being but one dimension that would arise from this acquisition as set forth in the 'Listing Particulars'.

I as Director, IT and Project Management (which included supply chain management) in the customer UK operating company was asked by Group towards the end of 1998 to additionally undertake the task of investigating the global aggregation opportunities with this key network infrastructure supplier in pursuit of cost synergy benefits. Being the co-leader (together with my supplier counterpart) of what became a globalization effort towards the realization of the cost synergies with this and later other suppliers, in July 2000 I transferred to the emerging customer global organization to focus entirely on these initiatives. This transfer later led to my appointment as the Director of Infrastructure Supply Chain Management in the customer global organization.

The first country quorum I engaged at an inaugural meeting in Newbury in February 1999 comprised the United Kingdom (in which I was working) as the lead network operator (having the greatest expenditure with the supplier) together with the Netherlands, Greece and Australia in each of which the customer had the majority equity interest, and together with their respective supplier in country partners. Today, this globalization initiative with this supplier organization has expanded to additionally include Albania, Egypt, Fiji, Germany, Ireland, Japan, Portugal, Romania, Spain and Switzerland; of importance to note is that the participation of all network operators (on the customer side) was and remains subject to a local management decision. We have, based upon the experiential learning of this project, launched comparable activities with other key cellular network infrastructure suppliers.

Given the geographic dispersion across time zones of the participant companies or operations of both organizations, I recognized that this transformation was being executed in a virtual organization and would also create a global virtual community. The need for an interorganizational information system (IS) capability, set initially at the strategic or interorganizational level (Bultje and van Wijk, 1998) and concerned with the co-operation between all the partners of the virtual organization was clear to me. At the inaugural Global Supply Chain Management (GSCM) meeting it was agreed to initiate a collaborative (or virtual) workstream led by the Netherlands, in which I later introduced a concept named *eRelationship* (Ibbott, 2001) through which to support the management of the global relationship that has since been operationalized and hosted by the supplier in Stockholm. It is a bi-directional portal between the organizations having over 5,000 registered users (at 31 December 2002), which importantly is n-dimensional among *all* of the companies within and between either organization; namely the virtual organization may comprise all companies of both organizations whether or not party to this specific relationship. Later some in-country customer–supplier relationships operationalized *eRelationship* for local initiatives, the operational level being concerned with the way individual partners carry out their own business processes (Bultje and van Wijk, 1998). Save confidential commercial information *eRelationship* is an open virtual environment consistent with the view of Lipnack and Stamps (1997: 228–229), 'open-book management that advocates providing essential information to everyone in the organization is one to contribute trust to the environment' and 'social capital is the "structure of relations between and among actors", individual or organization'.

The customer considers this transformational journey a success as it is contributing to the cost synergies as reported in the customer organization's interim results for six months to 30 September 2002:

> The globalization of the Group's supply chain relationships is advancing. The Group is now either managing or co-ordinating centrally the purchase of network infrastructure (including that related to 3G). Global supply chain management is generating significant synergy

savings for the Group . . . It is expected that the > £500m of forecast post tax cash flow synergies for the year ending March 2003 will be exceeded (for the declared scope of synergy activities).

Emergent issues for action

The business ambition of the customer was (and remains) clear, namely, to realize acquisition and process cost synergies for cellular network infrastructure through the aggregation of its network operating interests towards the manufacturers. This required both an interorganizational and inter-company relationship transformations of the pre-existing in-country customer–supplier relationships, all within a virtual organizational setting. This approach was new and (remains) unique in the cellular telecommunication industry and with no pre-existing organizational model to follow and therefore no transitional guidance.

It was clear to me that this process of global aggregation with one supplier would provide knowledge that the customer organization could use in similar relationships with other such suppliers. The transformational experiential learning was therefore studied more closely than otherwise might have been expected, and action has since been successfully taken to implement this model elsewhere.

The experiential journey

In late 1998, in advance of the merger, the customer resolved to assess the potential of cost synergies that could arise as a result thereof. One important area of significant Group expenditure, through which the potential to synergy realize benefits by aggregating operating company requirements, was the acquisition of cellular network infrastructure from common global suppliers.

The customer had the greatest such capital expenditure with the supplier in this study, which was therefore seen as a starting point for the pursuit of cost synergies. Following the appointment by the customer of myself as the leader for this endeavour, the supplier appointed as its global contact the most senior person in its UK Company (the General Managing Director), thereby encouraging the relationship to develop from a strong local historical background and a good personal relationship. We agreed to pursue a common strategy of the globalization of the interorganizational business relationship in those (products and services) areas wherein at least two operators shared an interest in common.

Prior to the ensuing transformation, the supply of cellular network infrastructure between the customer and the supplier was transacted under separately negotiated local commercial agreements in each country. While the network operators in which customer had an interest did communicate with each other, there was no attempt to align the network implementation of each country for combined benefit. Primary reasons included the fact that there was no structure within which to do so, each operator was focused on its own network rollout objectives, and there was no advantage at that time perceived by the supplier to aggregate and therefore no real motivation. These customer network operating companies serving local country markets were run and operated by the local in-country management team, with equity investment governance being executed by corporate offices (in the United Kingdom). The supplier's in-country operations on the other hand were subject to the rules of engagement established by the corporate organization and regional governance, but influenced by their local incentive business plans when establishing terms of business.

Hence all business was transacted at the local country level and subject to the locally negotiated and agreed terms and conditions. All local communication was direct (meaning non-mediated by corporate offices) through meetings, letters, emails, fax and telephone calls. Ordinarily, communication and meetings between the customer's equity interests and the supplier corporate units was mediated and arranged via the supplier's local subsidiary; it was normally the case that local supplier representation attended all customer meetings with corporate units. Figure 2.1 illustrates these relationship structures.

Stated differently, the supplier (in Sweden) viewed that the interorganizational relationships were multiple and 'owned' through each of their local country subsidiaries. The outcome of this approach was that equipment supplies to the customer (of configurations, pricing/terms and the processes) varied considerably across countries, giving rise to unnecessary costs for all parties, and lack of economic scale in production.

The transformation towards globalization

This joint globalization strategy was initiated in a joint meeting (subsequent meetings were called Global Supply Chain Management meetings) held in the United Kingdom in February 1999. Four operating interests in whom the customer had a majority equity position (United Kingdom, the Netherlands, Greece and Australia) were invited to join, together with their local supplier counterparts. During the initial period of the transformation and later arising from the merger, five other interests were invited to join what became known as the 'Supplier Club': Egypt, Germany, Portugal, Romania and Spain. The GSCM meeting participation grew over time, from an initial inclusive thirteen members (or actors) to fifty in the meeting at the end of the transformation, which included two directors from customer companies and four directors from the supplier's organization.

The inaugural GSCM meeting resolved that the joint activities would be conducted in an open and entirely transparent way in consideration of all

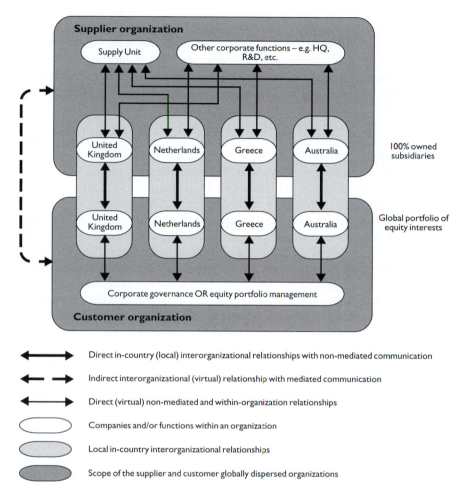

Figure 2.1 Initial customer–supplier interorganizational at commencement of globalization.

aspects of the processes and practices of either party from the point of sourcing until providing service to customers in country. A process-oriented journey (Orlikowski and Hofman, 1997) or experiential learning would prevail; there would be no requirement to produce plans that formed a rigid basis of workstream control.

The GSCM forum was not a traditional 'steering group'. Whereas steering groups are also forums where interested parties are represented, the role and line of reporting is often well defined. The GSCM was challenged with finding its role so as to realize joint benefits, having lines of reporting back to the customer and supplier organizations (through the actors of the forum) and varying as appropriate. However, it was accepted by all parties that the GSCM forum was the centre of collective leadership of the global transformation, albeit in a meta-influence dimension with respect to the operating companies. My supplier counterpart and I jointly led the GCSM forum although I was throughout the period more active in travelling the world, often together with another senior supplier person, to promote and motivate the customer operator and supplier interest in this endeavour.

The supplier translated the customer's primary motivation for the early realization of cost synergies into initial financial concessions. The complementary supplier motivation was to reduce the future costs of product definition, manufacture, rollout and distribution through the harmonization of the customer's product requirements. There was no classical agreement around the sharing of the cost reductions achieved, but simply that the benefits through process or practice improvements arising from the joint endeavours would be retained solely by the parties. The customer's equity based grouping required the concepts to be 'sold' to the management teams of each entity who had to decide to opt-in to the globalization endeavour, meaning a motivating business case or argument for the benefits of collaboration was a perquisite. For the supplier on the other hand, with fully owned subsidiaries, there was less scope to resist the propositions.

Through the GSCM meetings I tried to assure that the globalization programme would not be perceived as head office centric, and I sought to engage the global community. While the inaugural GSCM meeting was held in the United Kingdom, thereafter the venue variously moved to the Netherlands, Greece, Sweden, Egypt, Portugal, Romania and Spain. A further customer-only meeting to consider other supplier globalization opportunities was later held in Australia. The GSCM meetings were segmented into two parts, the separate customer and supplier pre-meetings followed by the joint forum; the customer pre-meeting played an increasingly important role in building the global community inclusive of aggregating and setting the priority of the combined (global) issues for the joint forum with supplier.

The GSCM meetings were supplemented by other modes of communication. I, in order to achieve the necessary commitment and investment of resources, visited the in-country executive management of both the customer and supplier. Such country visits around the world often included an accompanying senior contributor from supplier. I gave presentations to the senior global management of both organizations on globalization and eBusiness. Today the supplier sponsors the short publication of the 'Club News' for circulation in both organizations.

Virtual workstreams

My facilitation of the GSCM meetings resulted in the establishing of a number of *virtual workstreams* focusing on initiatives that were relevant for success; joint and collaborative activities that moved the relationship towards globalization. The leadership of these GSCM virtual workstreams were assigned in-country customer–supplier teams jointly, whose role it was to manage the progress of these initiatives and co-ordinate activities as required among all interested country operations. Having agreed the business logic of the globalization initiative, the virtual teams determine the next executable steps in the transformation process and the pace thereof. As the global collaboration model in Figure 2.2 illustrates (p. 33), the opportunity also existed and happened for virtual team collaboration independently within either organization and/or collaboration between the virtual teams of both organizations independently from the GSCM meeting.

The virtual teams had to resource and conduct operations from within their and the other interested country operations. This could be done as they saw fit – thus some teams arranged local workshops and other meetings; others operated on a largely virtual basis using email, the phone and (later) the developed IS. Further, each virtual team interacted with others as necessary. Virtual teams varied in size and the level of the actors within their own companies, both between teams and over time. Teams at points in time ranged from seven to eighteen members, and job titles included managing director, director, executive and others.

For those virtual workstreams initiated by the GSCM forum it was the case that the reporting on progress took place at GSCM meetings as appropriate, consensus on actions was affirmed and there was resolution regarding the construct and commitment of local resources to the virtual teams. The customer operators may choose to accept a lead role or otherwise opt for the role of participant (provide resources), observer or indeed stand back from the initiative; however, in each case they are obliged to the eventual outcome as determined by the GSCM forum.

Groupware and information systems

One of the vital virtual workstream initiatives was originally called *Group-ware*. The objective was to provide an information base that epitomized all aspects of the global interorganizational relationship and through which the constraints of time and geography were to be removed from the ability of the virtual teams to maintain positive contact on progress. This would be supplemented by phone calls, emails, the GSCM meetings, and whatever other meetings the virtual teams organized.

The stream was initially led by the Netherlands team, who had interest in and motivation for the required IS, and included the participation of the United Kingdom (and later Germany) and the supplier's corporate IS operation in Sweden. A steering group that met physically led the stream. Groupware was developed and implemented by the supplier, without budget discussions, and hosted on a supplier server in Sweden. A proposal from a large consulting firm to develop the IS for the customer–supplier relationship was rejected by the GSCM, in part due to the need to formalize requirements, but also due to questions over the consulting firm's ability to deliver a novel solution.

There now exists an n-way (meaning access by all companies of either organization) bi-directional portal through which all aspects of the customer–supplier relationship can be enacted, ranging from contract information through to downloads of software patches and selected product ordering. This concept was created and named by me as *eRelationship*, and this designation and vision has persisted into its operationalization by the supplier and is used by both organizations; the same model is under development in other such business relationships.

The informational content of most areas is managed directly by the contributors and not a central administration, or gatekeeper. Ownership of information such as manuals and instructions resides at source, reducing the risks of outdated information and local variations and copies. Like many intranet systems, the provision and arrangement of information are fluid. An exception to this is the ordering processes; all order processes are tested prior to implementation and are tightly managed.

There have been issues of an internal (to the two organizations) publication sponsored by the supplier under the headline 'Building the Customer–Supplier *eRelationship*' and this development has also featured in other internal customer publications. In the early days in support of the *eRelationship* activity the supplier also funded a promotional video for internal communication within the organizations.

Outcomes

In November 2002 I presented to a focus group of four executives from both organizations who were also actors in the transformation the IS Supported Transformational Interorganizational Organizational Model developed by me, and the Premises (to be discussed later) observed by me. This group was invited, as part of the analysis process, to comment on the findings and in fact provided further refinements that were incorporated in the results.

IS supported global collaboration model

Figure 2.2 illustrates the organizational arrangements that are now in-place to operate and advance the interorganizational relationship existing between the customer and supplier. The 'backbone' of the model is the Global Virtual Catalyst in the form of the GSCM meetings, comprising a multicultural global virtual community of actors drawn from the customer and supplier in country and central functions. These teams formed communities around virtual workstreams initiated in the GSCM meeting but also separately

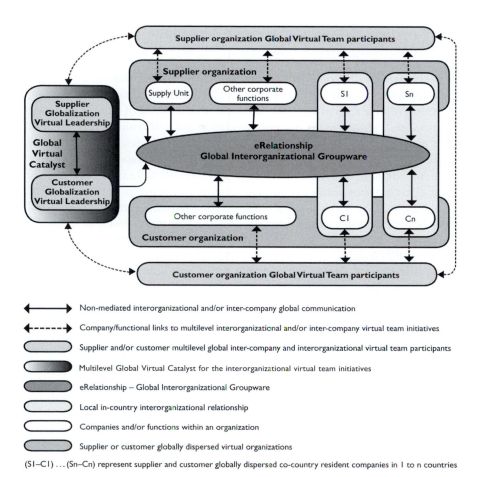

The following legend items appear below the diagram:

Non-mediated interorganizational and/or inter-company global communication

Company/functional links to multilevel interorganizational and/or inter-company virtual team initiatives

Supplier and/or customer multilevel global inter-company and interorganizational virtual team participants

Multilevel Global Virtual Catalyst for the interorganizational virtual team initiatives

eRelationship – Global Interorganizational Groupware

Local in-country interorganizational relationship

Companies and/or functions within an organization

Supplier or customer globally dispersed virtual organizations

(SI–CI) ... (Sn–Cn) represent supplier and customer globally dispersed co-country resident companies in 1 to n countries

Figure 2.2 IS supported global collaboration model (Ibbott, 2001: 222).

within and between the two organizations. The global virtual community while comprising actors of varying hierarchical positions in their originating companies conducted themselves in a non-hierarchical way. The GSCM meetings became like a gathering of long lost friends from around the world; through this strength which may be difficult to measure lay the fibre, tenacity and source of achievement of the total transformation programme; thereby suggesting that the balance of the richness of the various media was appropriate to the challenges of the organizational transformations being sought.

A relevant concept is that of *Teamnet*, which is defined as 'networks of teams that cross conventional boundaries and will improve horizontal organizational relationships whilst complementing or co-existing with the traditional prescriptions of vertical hierarchy; they cross boundaries and have fewer bosses and more leaders' (Lipnack and Stamps, 1993: 4); the GSCM meetings perhaps, and the virtual workstreams? Teamnets combine two organizational ideas, *teams* (where small groups of people work with focus, motivation, and skill to achieve shared goals), and *networks* (where disparate groups of people and groups 'link' to work together on a common purpose). Lipnack and Stamps (1993) go on to state that boundary crossing Teamnets offer a critical edge for dealing with the speed of change and new decentralised, globalized economy; this being derived from *power* (benefit from the power of the part *and* the power of the whole), *speed* (multiple decision-making leaders work in parallel on different aspects of the same problem – or goal, or common purpose) and *flexibility* (Teamnets are highly 'plastic' in that they configure and reconfigure to the needs of the moment). These teams, GSCM or virtual workstreams, manage virtually organized tasks beyond the individual organization (or company) level, in order to optimize the benefit for the entire network, or meta-management (Mowshowitz, 1997).

The intent of *eRelationship* is that it is not only intended to provide for transactions, but more importantly includes all information about the relationship between the customer–supplier organizations and their joint activities with the aim of neutralizing the impact of time and geographical location. This means that substantially all parties in either organization have the opportunity to work in the mutual interests on the basis of information in common. Only when the ability to transfer fragmented knowledge and expertise is achieved will the whole company (or combined organizations) be able to exploit the benefits of organizational learning. The information about or in one organization may be used to improve the performance of the other, or to improve relations between the organizations or the companies therein.

Reflections

A premise is a form of reflection in which one critiques the underlying assumptions and perspectives, and is an inquiry into the unstated and often-subconscious underlying assumptions that govern behaviour. In this case the context of the premises is at the strategic interorganizational level during the period of transition, and is as seen and experienced by the actors in the global interorganizational relationship as embedded variously in and between the local in-country and the interorganizational relationships of both organizations. The premises now follow.

Recognize the asymmetric nature of the synergy benefits

It is often the case in the initiation of a joint (customer–supplier) supply chain project with mutual benefits arising, that there is a debate as to the methodology of the sharing of the derived benefits. They are often a derivative of process improvements and ultimately cost benefits in the chain of supply in and between companies that are motivated by tactical or operational actions in contrast to being strategic outcomes. In this case however our business objective, the realization of cost synergies in the supply chain be they price or process cost, gave rise to our strategy to globalize the interorganizational relationship that became the focus of our business and transformational relationship activities thereafter. Key to our success, however, was that *the parties recognized that notwithstanding having a strategy in common (globalization), that there may be (and in fact was) an asymmetry in and timing of any ensuing benefits by either organization.* There was as a result no synergy benefit sharing agreement discussed or made at the commencement of the project, and there still is not. This permits either party to introduce initiatives either for self and/or mutual benefit anywhere in the supply process between what I referred to as 'source and service'; meaning through both organizations to the point of service delivery to the customer organization's end-customers and therefore revenue generation, as opposed to point of shipment ex-supplier factory.

Stimulation of the transformational momentum

The globalization in the supply chain in this case was a transformational endeavour, taking supplier companies who hitherto had separate (meaning uncoordinated or aggregated) and multiple interfaces to a common supplier and moving the interorganizational (customer–supplier) relationship to a harmonized or single primarily point of contact for those matters in common; this meant that the customer operators had to accede negotiations on those matters deemed global to a single company team (myself and team in the United Kingdom in this case). This situation was further complicated as the customer equity interests in its organization was various, while the complementary supplier companies were all 100 per cent owned subsidiaries. To avoid organizational resistance or pushback (particularly in the customer organization) *it was imperative therefore to provide a motivation to stimulate the momentum of the transformation.* Notwithstanding the aggregation of the customer requirements through a single interorganizational interface to the supplier for matters in common (primarily the acquisition of network infrastructure), the realization of the targeted synergies could be achieved only through the customer network operators, as it is they who actually place the purchase orders and not any central organization. The motivational catalyst, independent of the transformational approach, was (and remains) the pricing (and configuration) structures and associated global commercial terms and conditions, which together combine to deliver measurable benefits to the entire customer network operators; at least as the customer–supplier relationship evolved in this period. Clearly to the extent that price alone is in discussion and absent of any other changes a customer gain in the first instance would be a supplier loss; this serves to demonstrate the immediacy of the asymmetry. Further, this is reinforced through the participative approach taken by and organized through our global negotiating leadership. For all negotiated matters, no final commitment is made by the negotiating team to the supplier absent of consultation on the agreement of the supply chain community affected by the decision; this inclusive approach remains a key learning and a factor in the sustained success of this globalization approach. Ordinarily, the greater the scope of consultation so the perception of inhibiting the pace of progress prevails; in this case surprisingly the customer operator motivation was (and is) such as to reinforce the power of the decisions taken apparently with no adverse consequence to pace, even though the companies were acceding 'control' in these transformed circumstances.

Vested transformational leadership in management

As the customer sponsor for the globalization in the supply chain and the person accountable for the segment synergies, I engaged in global boundary crossing within both and between the two global organizations (customer and supplier) and at multilevels inclusive of the CEOs and members of the various company executive teams. The approach of being accountable for the synergy outcome through taking the thought leadership, communicating the message across the virtual community, building the relationships and trust with the executive of the businesses in which the synergies will be realized, and obtaining their commitment to the transformation, is different. This gave rise to the view that the *global sponsorship and boundary crossing leadership must be vested in person (or persons) responsible for management*. In these formative phases it is perhaps relevant to note that I was Director in the lead customer company for this initiative. Daft (2000) summarizes that transformational leaders are

> characterized by the ability to bring about change, innovation, and entrepreneurship. Transformation leaders motivate followers not just to follow them personally but (also) to believe in the vision of corporate transformation, to recognize the need for revitalization, to sign on for the new vision, and help institutionalize the new organization process.
>
> (Daft, 2000: 507)

It has been my experience in this and the later application of this transformational model with other vendors, that while I retain an overall commercial governance role that there a number of 'followers' very well able to convey the message and enact success in a comparable way with this and now other suppliers albeit that I retain the role of the executive communication; perhaps a challenge for succession?

Collective anchor for successful transformation

The interorganizational and inter-company transformational backbone was a forum that had the function of being a Global Virtual Catalyst, namely, the Global Supply Chain Management meetings. It comprised representation from each (customer and supplier) in-country company and the global leadership of both organizations that included selectively corporate participation. The meeting format was that the first half day or so were separate caucuses followed by up to a day and a half in joint sessions; this facilitated two evening sessions/dinners that provided for extensive global networking within and between both organizations, thereby leading to a non-hierarchical global community. The venue, by request of the country teams, was by rotation hosted in the forum member countries throughout this period of research. This forum set and monitored a number of targeted (by mutual agreement) supply chain virtual workstreams each of which had a country (joint customer and supplier) leadership working collectively with other interested counties. The success of this approach, which has since been effective in other supplier relationships since, gives rise to the learning *that for an effective interorganizational and inter-company relationship transformation a joint customer–supplier non-hierarchical Global Virtual Catalyst should be established as the collective anchor for the transformation objectives*. The evidence also demonstrated that while this forum did not have a structural role in the participating companies (the vertical hierarchy), it did nevertheless through this catalytic forum and its actors in the horizontal relationships sufficiently influence the practice and views therein so as to achieve the collective or aggregate objectives – the meta-influence wherein the participants are motivated by an objective in common. These roles through the horizontal relationships between companies within and/or either between organization are in effect forms of meta-management. Meta-management is defined as the management of virtually organized tasks, beyond the individual organization (or company) level, in order to optimise the benefit for the entire network (Mowshowitz, 1997). This realization of not just indirect influence within the companies of both organizations, but actually aspiring to a positive synergy result (the object in this case) through the meta-influence was a powerful learning experience for me. The reality was that the catalyst (the GSCM forum) had developed an engaged multicultural and multilevel (hierarchically) with sufficient motivation to take back to their companies argument and motivated (economic) rationale for change in areas that were not of their direct responsibilities either.

Multi-company and organization virtual teaming

This journey was one in which the outcomes were not known at the commencement of the virtual team activities thereby making it an incremental journey through which effective pace was realized in a radical transformation (Gallivan *et al.*, 1994; Orlikowski, 1996; Orlikowski and Hofman, 1997). The virtual team approach was fully inclusive (customer and supplier organizations and the companies therein), albeit stimulated by the globalization vision, and united through the agreed objectives in common. It is important to note that the virtual teams were primarily drawn from country organizations within which the actual changes would need to occur, and supported by more centrally based resource that also provided the governance through the Global Virtual Catalyst. This approach supported the proposition *that for a successful interorganizational and inter-company transformation in a global virtual environment leadership of virtual teams should be allocated jointly to the customer and supplier in-country companies.* Of importance to note here is that my leadership contribution was that while I offered a vision (or thought leadership), there was and remains no grand plan to which everyone has to perform; my expectation is that had that been the case the endeavour would most likely have been a failure. Through my chosen inclusive approach, meaning to test the response to rational business objectives and to seek support for each (virtual team) initiative, I enabled an inclusive and consultative approach within which the teams themselves resolved the art of the possible with the support of others within their respective companies, such that while not always aspiring to what I may have wanted in a single step, nevertheless moved the 'game' on.

The dynamics of leadership versus observer/contributor

It was our experience that the initial assignment of the leadership of a virtual team did not necessarily assure the desired progress and/or result therefore giving rise to the need to reassign the virtual team leadership continuity to another country team. Such reasons included exhausting the skill set and resource availability locally, the need to involve more central resource and commitment to achieve the team objective, and the lead country not being appropriately central to the critical mass of implementation even though they had successfully mobilized the initiative. We carried out changes of leadership without developing any tensions that may otherwise have occurred if the concept of a fixed centre of excellence approach had been taken; in this case and with the assignments allocated, the flexibility was derived with the participants and their companies and did not require the redeployment of fixed assets. The learning being that to be effective in a supply chain with an interorganizational and inter-company transformation in a global virtual environment, *that there is an acceptance of the fluidity of either sometimes leading the Global Virtual Team initiatives, or the following the lead of others either as a contributor or as an observer* (an elected option by some companies). This outcome is consistent with the notion that in virtual teams of the systematic ability to switch satisfiers in a decision environment of bounded rationality (Mowshowitz, 1997). My learning was that just as there is a danger in prescribing the required transformational steps for success as discussed earlier, there too is a risk particularly in transition to assume that leadership (or the designated 'satisfier') is fixed for all time; the assignment of 'satisfier' should be reviewed from time to time.

Coevolution of interorganizational IS, eRelationship

As the country customer and supplier participants were being obliged in the transformational paradigm to accede control of hitherto local activities to the virtual workstreams, it was agreed with me that we needed to create an 'as though you were here' (virtual) environment; meaning that all actors and colleagues should have time-independent and non-mediated access of all current global activities should they require it, inclusive of a transactional capability. This gave rise to the introduction by me of the concept of *eRelationship*, the pilot for which was (and still is) hosted by the supplier in Sweden. The agreement was that any person in either of the customer or supplier organizations may have access to all aspects of this bi-directional portal whether or not they were engaged in this particular business relationship, save only the limitation of access to a subset in commercially sensitive areas like pricing, volumes and commercial terms – an open approach. As stated elsewhere this initiative commenced with only a conceptual statement of requirement, no plans and no budget and has since coevolved (meaning 'the evolution of two or more interdependent species (or activities), each adapting to changes in the other': *American Heritage Dictionary of the English Language*, fourth edition) through and with the participation of the country operations and continues to be hosted by the supplier. The learning here being *that to achieve an effective interorganizational and inter-company relationship transformation in a global supply chain that a joint customer and supplier Global Virtual Team be established to incrementally progress the implementation of an eRelationship capability.* As in this case one should first focus on the operationalization at the strategic interface level and be flexible at the country level in the implementation of operational interfaces (Bultje and van Wijk, 1998); companies have collaborated on projects locally in-country towards the operation of *eRelationship* to their own ends.

Conceptual generalizations

This rich case study has only been proven within the supply chain between two globally structured (although differently) organizations. Implementation has successfully commenced in three other major similar supplier relationships using the same transformational organizational model. Conceptually it is the case however my view is that this approach may be taken in any transformational or co-operative endeavour in a virtual organizational situation, be it within one organization with companies or branches or teams in multiple locations within or between countries, or indeed between multiple organizations variously geographically situated; to be definitive however more research is required. Both the IS supported global collaboration model shown in Figure 2.2 and the premises highlighted from my practitioner experience provide a positive experiential learning towards success in the other vendor relationship initiatives now under-way and those conceptual thoughts discussed.

While the model shown in Figure 2.2 describes and portrays the nature of the variant relationships it does not in my view demonstrate the relationship dynamics (as is the case in many models), trust and the motivation factors for entity or individual participation and may therefore be considered a passive representation. The literature on the other hand makes reference to three constituent components that have been relevant in my analysis to the stimulation and motivation in achieving the transformation described; namely, trust between all parties, positive relationships and mutually respected motivation.

Trust is the crucial defining feature of a virtual collaboration (Ishaya and Macaulay, 1999), the qualified environment in this case study. Trust is defined as a characteristic for collaboration where members believe in the character, ability, integrity, familiarity and morality of each other (Ishaya and Macaulay, 1999). An alternative (but nevertheless consistent) definition by Ring and Van de Ven (1994) of trust is that as an individual's confidence in the goodwill of the others in a given group, and the belief that the other's will make efforts consistent with the group's goals. This case evidence supports that by these definitions trust was present given, for example, the positive functioning of the virtual teams that were led (by mutual consent) by a single country local group on behalf of the overall group, and similarly in my case in assuming the global commercial negotiation lead responsibilities on behalf of the collective that required the local operators to accede direct control of certain negotiations. In the relationship with the supplier, the fact that there was an acceptance mutually and no mechanism through which to share benefits was never an item for discussion.

Organizational identification may be the critical glue linking virtual workers and organizations. Through its impact on employee's motivations, organizational identification facilitates coordination and control. The literature suggests that the strength of identification determines some critical beliefs and behaviours; interpersonal trust, the desire to remain with the organization, the willingness to co-operate with others, to accept organizational goals as their own, and the willingness to perform extra-role behaviours. In this case the creation of the global virtual community or group identity was key, as was the positive decision to rotate the hosting venue for the GSCM meeting among the 'Club' member countries, which enhanced the national pride as the hosting too became a competitive event. As a relevant adjunct, 'Open-book management that advocates providing essential information to everyone in the organization is one to contribute trust to the environment' and 'Social capital is the "structure of relations between and among actors", individual or organization' (Lipnack and Stamps, 1997: 228–229); a concept supported in the approach taken with *eRelationship*, the IS support capability.

From a relationship and motivation perspective it is also important, in my experience, to invest in face-to-face time for the start up and launch phases (of the virtual team), reserve time for meetings to assess team progress, create breakpoints where the team converges and realigns its work, and celebrate success (Lipnack and Stamps, 1997) which in part was an indirect role of the GSCM forum (it had its fun side too). Nutt and Backoff (1997: 506) state that a (an organizational) transformation is more likely (to be successful) when leaders empower (or delegate to) key people and trust them to find ways to realize a vision through development of team activities (or virtual workstreams, in my case study); specifically, with respect to leaders, they say that in their approach leaders should be 'on tap, but not on top'.

In this case study the GSCM meetings supported by the separate virtual teams has been a cornerstone for the social networking, the delegation of trust and the (distributed) empowerment or leadership delegation in the interests of the collective. Further, in support of the approach taken in the case, to allow the global company to integrate as many of its functions over time, distance, and culture without resorting to the stifling power of centralization, regular face-to-face meetings to break down interpersonal barriers, and develop networks of people who trust each other based on personal relationships; the emphasis here being the personal relationships, which is consistent with a notion of the building of trust between the actors. It is worthy to note that shared confidence (and trust) among those who work across organizational boundaries create an environment for inter-unit support, which again is evidenced in all the central virtual activities, i.e. the GSCM meetings, and the virtual teams with workstream assignments on behalf of the collective. What is key to recognize from the case data and my experience in the horizontal relationships between the customer–supplier organizations, and between companies within either organization, is the consistency of the multilevel positions of the actors engaged in the virtual group exchanges, which may be considered to have visibly (to all the actors) strengthened the commitment and resolve to success (or at least removes the element of decision and doubt) for both organizations.

A novel aspect of this case is the customer equity ownership positions; when one organization does not comprise of wholly owned subsidiaries introduces a further and potentially unique complexity. Issues of trust arise not only between organizations (customer and supplier in this case), but also between the operating interests of the customer. The customer has to persuade and engage, rather than direct its various parts, generating motivation across its equity interests.

Finally, radical change in the context of this case is that 'radical change replaces the status quo with a new order of things and as a result may create serious disruptions in structures, processes, operations, knowledge, and morale' (Gallivan *et al.*, 1994: 325). While based on a single field study, involving the implementation of a set of integrated CASE tools at a large chemical products company, at two points in time (which may be a limitation) it was shown that gradual implementation of radical change may not only be feasible, but also effective in some situations; a relevant perspective in this case too given the nature and dynamics of the transformations and the approach taken. The conclusion is, in the words of Gallivan *et al.* (1994: 337) 'the pace of implementing change (rapid versus gradual) should be distinguished, at least conceptually, from the nature of change intended (radical versus incremental), and the two considered separate choices for the change agent'.

References

Bultje, R. and van Wijk, J. (1998) Taxonomy of Virtual Organizations, based on definitions, characteristics and typology. *virtual-organization.net Newsletter.* http://www.virtual-organization.net/files/articles/nl2–3.pdf

Daft, R. L. (2000) *Organization Theory and Design.* South-Western College Publishing, Cincinnati, OH.

Gallivan, M. J., Hofman, J. D. and Orlikowski, W. J. (1994) Implementing Radical Change: Gradual Versus Rapid Pace. Paper give to *Fifteenth International Conference on Information Systems*, pp. 325–339.

Ibbott, C. J. (2001) An IS-Enabled Model for the Transformation and Globalisation of Interorganisational and Inter-Company Relationships. Doctor of Business Administration, Henley Management College, Brunel University, Uxbridge, UK.

Ishaya, T. and Macaulay, L. (1999) The Role of Trust in Virtual Teams. *virtual-organization.net Newsletter.* http://www0.virtual-organization.net/News/NL_Special_Issue99/Ishaya_US.pdf

Lipnack, J. and Stamps, J. (1993) *The TeamNet Factor: Bringing the Power of Boundary Crossing into the Heart of your Business.* Oliver Wright Publications, Essex Junction, VT.

Lipnack, J. and Stamps, J. (1997) *Virtual Teams: Reaching across Space, Time, and Organizations with Technology.* John Wiley and Sons, New York.

Mowshowitz, A. (1997) Virtual Organization, *Communications of the ACM*, 40(9): 30–37.

Nutt, P. C. and Backoff, R. W. (1997) Facilitating Transformational Change, *Journal of Applied Behavioral Science*, 33(4): 490–508.

Orlikowski, W. J. (1996) Improvising Organizational Transformation over Time: A Situated Change Perspective, *Information Systems Research*, 7(1): 63–92.

Orlikowski, W. J. and Hofman, J. D. (1997) An Improvisational Model for Change Management: The Case of Groupware Technologies, *Sloan Management Review*, 38(2): 11–21.

Ring, P. S. and Van de Ven, A. H. (1994) Developmental Processes of Cooperative Interorganizational Relationships, *Academy of Management Review*, 19(1): 90–118.

Chapter 3

Taking charge of a mature family business

Derek Whelan

Background and context

This chapter tells the story of how I took up the role of CEO of a small to medium-sized family business in the period 1993–1994. In 1961, following completion of an on-the-job apprenticeship, the family business ('the business') was founded by my father ('the founder') as a mechanical repair shop. Over time the business incrementally developed into importation, distribution and repair services for mechanical engineering equipment. By 1993 the company had come through more than one financial crisis and despite having grown in its early years it had now plateaued. Sales had remained static for five years.

As the eldest son I grew up living and knowing but not working in the business. Throughout the long formative years, the business concerns were always brought home. They were the cause of many tensions, as pressures regularly spilled into family life. All knew of and often shared the sleepless nights and the reasons behind them. It was regularly a topic of conversation at the family table. Products were stored in the garage. Paperwork was processed in the home. Business meetings were regularly held in family rooms.

Upon graduating from college in 1978 it was expected that I would join the business. However, I declined and commenced a career which included completion of several professional qualifications (specializing in finance and in corporate turnaround) and, ultimately, progression to multinational board level abroad. By 1992 my two younger brothers had been employed within the firm for fifteen years since leaving school. They rotated through various roles until they eventually settled into activities within which they felt comfortable. As family members they were titled 'company directors'. Succession planning was never openly or frankly discussed within the family. The issue was an uncomfortable one for the founder. However, throughout their working years in the business, my brothers were encouraged to believe, and consequently presumed, that succession would ultimately be decided in their joint favour. By 1992, nearing the age of 60 and having long contemplated the succession issue, without any external advice my father concluded that neither of his two long-serving sons nor any other member of his management team had the broad business skills necessary to further develop the business. He believed that none could adequately assume his role as chief executive. In 1992 he shared his thoughts on retiring with me. The business pressures were too much. He could not cope. He wanted out. We discussed possibilities such as an external sale of the business, which he disliked. We discussed his retention of the business but managed by a totally external appointment, but he really wanted to keep the senior role within the family. He had nobody to fill his position as CEO. He believed I was suited. Therefore, he said, the 'job was there' if I wanted it. The matter should not be discussed with anyone, he requested, until I made a decision. At that time, he would explain everything to my brothers and other directors within the business.

I felt obliged to respond; to continue the family business; to help my father. Inwardly I believed the business had real but undeveloped potential. However, the risks concerned me. I was unsure how my brothers would feel about my joining; unsure whether to expect a warm welcome or cold resentment from them and other directors; unsure if surrendering my overseas career was worth the sacrifice. I also strongly suspected that the business was in trouble. If my suspicions were correct, I wondered if one individual could make a difference. A year later, in 1993, these and many other questions were to the forefront in my mind as I resigned from my overseas employment to return home to take up the role and the challenge. On arriving home, I was collected from the airport by my father. I asked how my brothers and the other company directors had responded to his announcement regarding retirement and my appointment as CEO. They had not yet been told, he said. He could not find the words.

My father asked that I arrange a meeting for the following month at which he would announce his retirement decision and my appointment as CEO. In the interim, I was asked to remain silent. Upon arriving at the business, I discovered family and staff had been led to believe that I was returning to help identify and resolve financial difficulties which had recently emerged. During the following month a full financial analysis by me confirmed that the business was on the verge of failure. Cash reserves were gone, turnover was static, margins were in decline and overheads were rocketing. As management accounts had never been prepared, this situation was a genuine shock to the others. This crisis was presented by me to the first collective meeting of my father, brothers and other company directors. Then, at the close of the meeting, my father paused and said he had an announcement to make regarding his retirement and my appointment as CEO. The pause continued silently for several minutes until he finally turned to me and asked that I make the announcement on his behalf. He still could not find the right words. Uproar followed. This was an unacceptable development. They would not agree. My father asked that all should consider the gravity of the financial crisis the business faced and insisted that positive and constructive support be given. Following heated exchanges, to a visibly reluctant gathering of brothers and other company directors, my role as CEO was confirmed.

The issues

Over the following weeks and following intensive investigation, analysis and discussion, it quickly became apparent there were several key issues:

- Many items for decision were likely to arise in a very short time-frame.
- The immediate and most pressing issue was the financial crisis. If it were not speedily resolved, everything else would be irrelevant.
- I suspected radical change was necessary. To create a successful, reshaped and rejuvenated organization it would be necessary to quickly identify and understand the external and internal forces at work, and to identify and implement solutions.
- Unknown levels of internal resistance, from all sources, had to be anticipated.

A model for taking charge

Gabarro (1985, 1987) provided a template against which I could pace my progress. I found his predictions regarding actions and stages that all newcomers must go through following a new appointment had significant parallels to my own situation. Based on a study of a number of firms where new general managers had been appointed, he identified five predictable stages, each of roughly six months in duration, which together comprised the 'taking charge' process of a new manager. These are summarized in Table 3.1. I believed it would be interesting to learn from, test and apply his proposed sequence of 'taking charge' events. First, it might prompt me to undertake actions that I could otherwise overlook. Second, it would indicate to me whether I was leading or lagging in my own pace of personal and organizational development. Finally, it would test if my situation was part of a predictable pattern, which would alter my original belief (and possibly the common view held by all new managers) that I was experiencing a situation without precedent. The major lessons were learned throughout the first two phases of 'taking hold ' and 'immersion' and the remainder of this chapter will concentrate on telling the story and the lessons learned on reflection following each of those two phases.

Phase I: taking hold

Gabarro (1985) held that the taking hold stage typically lasted from three to six months and was characterized by a period of intense action, learning,

Table 3.1 A summary of the predicted characteristics through the total taking-charge process

Phase	Predicted timetable	Predicted characteristics by phase
Taking hold	Sept. 1993–Feb. 1994	Intense action and learning; quick corrective actions, problem fixing; impact of prior experience
Immersion	Mar. 1994–Aug. 1994	Dramatic decrease in changes: high learning and understanding
Reshaping	Sept. 1994–Feb. 1995	Increased level of reconfiguration activity and organizational change
Consolidation	Mar. 1995–Aug. 1995	Residual identification and resolution of new and unanticipated problems
Refinement	Sept. 1995–Feb. 1996	End of taking charge period; incremental and routine learning; the search for new opportunities

Source: based on Gabarro (1985).

evaluation and orientation which often set the tone and the direction for the remainder of the taking charge process. Based on prior experience and speed of learning in the new position, Gabarro wrote that newcomers would fix such problems as they could and that actions in this phase would tend to be of a corrective nature.

As my investigation into the affairs of the business progressed, I soon discovered the organization's financial crisis was a manifestation of what later emerged to be a more deep-seated issue – external, internal and other conditions had significantly changed over a prolonged period but management had not matched, responded or even recognized these shifts. It appeared that crisis management was required.

In the first six months a programme of change (radical, when compared to prior years of no change whatsoever) was launched. This included letting go unproductive staff; overhead cost cutting; remuneration restructuring based on individualized target achievements; aggressive marketing and promotion of core business strengths; renegotiations with key suppliers and buyers. Management and staff had no experience of managing change and there was manifest reluctance to embrace change by all and sundry. This coupled with the urgency of the situation forced me to implement the changes single-handedly. Many were difficult and unpopular decisions. Coercion of necessity appeared to be the required management style and from my experience of change management seemed the right way to proceed. Gabarro (1985) had predicted that:

> Managers' functional backgrounds, managerial experiences and special competencies appear to determine how they take charge, what actions they take and how competently they implement them . . . (and for new

managers studied) their initial actions were in areas where they had functional experience.

(Gabarro, 1985: 116)

Gabarro (1987) later reinforced his opinion about the impact of prior experience:

All other things being equal, prior experience, especially during the taking-hold stage, was the *single most powerful factor* associated with what the new manager focused on, the changes he made and the competencies of his early actions.

(Gabarro, 1987: 39)

As I saw it, the financial crisis was in need of urgent attention. The quickest solutions to implement were all financial in nature, most were internal, and all were within my experience base and comfort zone.

Phase I: taking hold – reflections and lessons

Could the changes have been handled differently? I believed at the time that the time factor alone did not allow for anything other than immediate action. Nevertheless, with hindsight and on reflection, had time been available I would have handled change differently in that first phase.

The first observation was that I had not canvassed to see whether there would, or would not, be widespread support for radical change. My presumption had been that communication of the financial crisis and of the change measures to be implemented only to family and other company directors would be enough. My rationale was that I wanted to avoid creating panic and fear within the remainder of the organization, possibly leading to an external leakage of the problems faced by the organization and also the consequent potential loss of key staff. As it ultimately transpired, resistance emerged at all levels from family and other directors and key staff members. Many of the change actions impacted areas where business directors had held responsibility; the change actions were regarded as interference and intrusions into their domains. The lesson learned was that the crisis should have been communicated to all staff members and support sought. Natural leakage, coupled with exaggerated and distorted communication from family members, spread an apocalyptic version of the emerging crisis in any event. This in turn created a barrier; long-serving directors and managers felt they should have been trusted and more deeply involved in the change implementation.

The second observation was that I should not have tried to do it all myself. The lesson learned was that if support had been solicited, the personal pressure to achieve so much in so little time might have been lessened. Also the potential for bond-building through a united defence and through common ownership of a solution against a common enemy would have been there.

The third observation concerned my initial discovery that the full extent of my role had not been communicated by my father to my brothers and other organization staff. The level of difficulty remained high due to the failure of the founder to communicate, establish and clarify my role earlier to both the family and the organization: 'top management can take a number of steps to help minimise [these] problems. The most obvious of these is making the new person's charter explicit' (Gabarro, 1985: 122).

The fourth observation was my presumption that once the confusion was settled, when a change programme was underway and when tangible results started to flow to the clear benefit of both individuals and the company, the organization would settle down. Certainly the initial outburst of resistance reduced once the financial crisis was broadly communicated, when my role and intentions were clarified and measurable, and particularly when visible and favourable results started to flow.

But after a period of about four months, major resistance began to surface. My brothers, I learned, now appreciated the longer term impact of what had occurred and had begun to mobilize the support of others affected by the changes. Thus began a prolonged period of intense sibling rivalry, coupled with growing pressure on my father to reverse his retirement intention and succession decision. However, in March 1994, six months into my role, my father announced he was retiring at end of the month.

Phase II: immersion

By early 1994 I had arrived at the beginning of the 'immersion' period which Gabarro (1985) wrote could last from four to eleven months, the actual time depending on the nature of learning and action that characterized the stage. Gabarro (1985) commented:

> the immersion period is quiet . . . during which executives acquire greater understanding of their new situations . . . new managers run the organization in a more informed fashion and steep themselves in a less hectic, finer grained learning process . . . arriving at a better understanding of the more basic dynamics of the organization, people and the industry.
>
> (Gabarro, 1985: 113)

Due to the more focused learning and understanding gained during this period, Gabarro wrote that this would result in the development of a different concept of what needed to be done or at least in a considerably modified notion of how the organization could be made more effective. I began to search for help and undertook extensive research through the management literature to find insights and/or solutions to the issues I was facing.

Immersion in relevant literature

Literature abounded with endorsements of my suspicions and future difficulties. Some of the ideas from my reading which added most to my level of understanding are now detailed.

First, management was guilty of a systematic failure of organizational strategy to keep pace with environmental change, which Johnson (1987: 33) described as 'strategic drift'. The organization had entered a 'paradigmatic state' (Sheldon, 1980) in which it adjusted only marginally within the reigning management paradigm but in fact had ceased to adapt to changes in the environment. Dunphy and Stace (1988: 320) described conditions of 'environmental creep' where the environment was changing incrementally but in ways imperceptible to managers, and 'organizational creep' where the organization itself moved out of strategic alignment with an environment which remained relatively stable.

Second, in order to immediately address these issues I had instinctively and rapidly moved into a turnaround mode delivered through a coercive or dictatorial transformation style, as described by Dunphy and Stace (1988). However, Dunphy and Stace (1992) in a later paper did warn that:

> Toughness for its own sake is an insufficient rationale for this type of change. It is often emotionally enervating on the leaders and the workforce. However . . . if the organization is at a low level of performance and if support for major change is low, it may be kinder on the organization to act decisively, to take the pain quickly, than to linger on over years trying to make changes incrementally.
>
> (Dunphy and Stace, 1992: 9)

Baden-Fuller and Stopford (1992) also wrote:

> Like frightened rabbits transfixed in the headlights of an approaching vehicle, mature organisations often perceive that something must be done, yet they are mesmerised and paralysed. Death for the rabbit may be swift, but for the mature organisation it is often a long period of unexciting financial results and strategic failures until crisis forces [closure].
>
> (Baden-Fuller and Stopford, 1992: 92)

Finally, my efforts to change the organization arose from a belief that the organization would, or should, be able to perform better. But I was becoming reluctant to *force* change, because of increasing negative reactions to the coercive style of change I had originally adopted. After all, the organization could not be directed to change. I could not mandate change. Rather I increasingly wanted to *encourage* change and create an environment where change would be possible, where change would emerge, or where change could be fostered.

Romanelli and Tushman (1994) offered hope regarding my aspiration:

> those who come from outside organisations stand uncommitted to the strategies and policies established by their predecessors . . . their information and experience may lead them to have different under-standings of effective or appropriate organizational actions . . . [and] begin work in an atmosphere of expectancy about change. The periods closely following their installation provide the best opportunity for signalling that the new regimes are in place.
>
> (Romanelli and Tushman, 1994: 1145)

The diagnosis which I carried out as part of this second phase is detailed under a number of headings. The first of these was identifying areas for change.

Immersion in identifying suitable change targets

I now needed to determine what sort of areas should be subject to change and within these, what the change priorities should be. The detailed analysis is not reproduced here but a summary of the main areas for change is repro-duced in Box 3.1. As can be seen even the summary list is a long one.

Immersion in culture

Having completed the above exercise, and in conjunction with events becoming a little less frenetic, it was evident that cultural forces were probably the single most powerful obstacles to progress. Consequently most of the remainder of this chapter focuses on cultural issues.

There were twin cultural forces in action, sometimes overlapping, some-times independent, sometimes combined:

- The 'family' culture, which separately arose from outside and inside the business. My father had retired in deed but not in act and was readily accessible to my brothers (the 'external family' culture). My two brothers shared my father's beliefs and also shared sets of their own (the 'internal family' culture).
- A 'normal internal organization' culture also arose from non-family directors and staff.

By 1994 the environment had continued to change and had recently become more unstable, yet the culture had been well established over fifteen years

Environmental level	Organizational level
1 Competitors	1 Twin cultures: organization and family
2 Industry structure	
3 Entry + exit requirements	2 Strategies, goals + planning
4 Technical	3 Technology
5 Buyers	4 Process + procedures
6 Suppliers	5 Task designs
7 Market niches + new opportunities	6 Structure
	7 Competencies
8 Regulation	8 Product mix
9 The family	

Interpersonal and group level	Individual level
1 Leadership styles	1 Motivation
2 Power + politics	2 Commitment
3 Authority relationships	3 Performance
4 Conflict management styles	4 Attitudes
5 Group composition	5 Skills and abilities
6 Group cohesiveness	6 Position
7 Sibling rivalry	7 Number + type of employees

Box 3.1 A categorization of potential change targets within the firm.

without any significant deliberate or conscious change. It was well out of balance with the environment. Unconscious change had certainly occurred within the organization over time because the founder, from 1986 onwards, had moved to a level of *active semi-retirement*. Of particular relevance was the fact that no capable leader had been delegated or trained to act in his place during those years. There was also no professional management employed. During the years to 1993 the founder was regularly away from the business more often than in attendance and became increasingly uninterested. Consequently, for a prolonged period, the organization had little leadership, direction, planning or control.

With no co-ordination the organization had fragmented and 'the whole' had reduced itself to the sum of its parts. Power players had emerged to develop their own 'fragment' to best suit themselves. Due to the absence of leadership and control, a culture had developed that everybody was free to do their own thing without interference from and without explanation to anyone. A team spirit was present but was totally unfocused in practice. Teams were formed by the individuals themselves to attack important tasks rather than by direction or co-ordination. The composition would depend on who happened to be available on the day, rather than who was best suited to the task.

During this time the general dominance of 'the family' remained well established. The family had not acted to halt the demise of the business mainly because they did not perceive a problem and, even if they had (other than the founder) would not have had the authority, skills or knowledge to do anything about it.

Immersion in identification of twin cultures: business and family

Twin culture problems therefore had to be tackled: the organization culture proper and, separately, the family culture. The first family problem arose through the failure of my father to communicate to my two brothers, and indeed the organization, his intention to retire and his replacement by me as CEO.

> Selecting a successor can often mean choosing between sons or daughters who, until now, have all been harbouring their own secret ambitions of succeeding when their father retires; and the father himself is often ambivalent about succession because he is worried about the ability of his children and how he is to approach favouring one at the expense of the others.
>
> (Smyth and Leach, 1993: 17)

Naturally this did not help me. Therefore, I recognized that the family would have to be separately managed as a distinct significant group with its own culture and certainly more expressive in its feelings and expectations regarding entitlements, perks, privileges and the like. By March 1994 twin cultures had been long established within the organization and were typified by the separate attitude and value systems that were then evident. I have summarized these in Table 3.2.

It was against this background that the first visible signs of family reaction emerged against my coercive change style. My brothers complained bitterly that change was happening too quickly and they were unhappy that they did not know what was going on. They wanted to be informed in advance of every significant change that I anticipated in order that they could give their considered opinion. They wanted to be part of the decision-making process. They wanted the right to veto decisions that they might be unhappy with.

They were advised that this could not happen due to the urgency of the broad range of decisions that had to be made, most being made on the spot and without the luxury of time. They were reminded that the organization was in a crisis. But rather than accept this, they enlisted the support of the founder and also the organization (non-family members) to press home their demands. The founder, emotionally unwilling to make logical and unemotional decisions, started to side with my brothers. The founder still believed in his 'family before business' philosophy and disagreed with my

Table 3.2 Family versus organization: attitude and value summary

Value	Family	Organization
Remuneration	Take whatever you need	Earnings based on effort
Promotion	Family members have a right to a directorship	Based on contribution to developing the business
Vacation	Open-ended and unaccountable	Fixed and accountable
Effort expectation	Do your best	Predetermined achievement targets
Equity ownership	Keep it within the family	No predetermined scheme
Capabilities	Move family members around until something is found that each individual is suited to	Must meet role expectations
Recruitment	Provide opportunities to relatives in need	Recruit externally and only as needed

opinion that business should come before family. He also regarded his support for their requirements as a compromise, to placate my brothers, who were still angry that neither of them had been given the role of CEO.

> Unfortunately, experience shows that most entrepreneurial fathers, even when they understand the processes that are at work, are not good at getting to grips with their dilemma themselves . . . their fears . . . make it difficult for them to grasp that there may be valid alternative points of view which they can accept . . . this means that much of the responsibility for taking positive action falls on the son's shoulders.
>
> (Smyth and Leach, 1993: 63)

Events as described confirmed my earlier conclusion that both cultures, in the form of 'the family' and 'the organization', would have to be separately managed. On a day-to-day basis the cultures behaved independently. But in the event of a disagreement they were variously independent and united, the form being determined by whichever would best provide maximum leverage to the aggrieved party on the day.

Immersion in understanding the determinants of culture

Schein (1983) defined culture as:

> the sum total of the collective or shared learning [of a group] as it develops its capacity to survive in its external environment and to

manage its own internal affairs. Culture is the solution to external and internal problems which have worked consistently for a group and are therefore taught to new members as the correct way to perceive, think about and feel in relation to those problems.

(Schein, 1983: 3)

Williams *et al.* (1993) elaborated on notable characteristics of culture. Culture was learned from an internal and external environment common to the members. It was both an input and an output, as managers, having been members of an organization for some time, both set and became products of the culture. It therefore became self-perpetuating and highly resistant to change. It was also partly unconscious, was historically based, was commonly held rather than shared and was heterogeneous.

As of March 1994, I saw the family, in combination with the founder, as an external *and* internal force. The family was acting to keep the organization unchanged as a family dominated business entity. To me this force was as significant as any other environmental influence creating a need for change. Note that 'the author' is represented as being outside the established patterns of behaviour because in March 1994 I still regarded myself to be 'untainted' by these.

By early 1994 it was apparent that change was required on a broad basis and that culture could be used either to achieve both existing and future change initiatives and objectives or, alternatively, that the culture(s) would destroy them. The immediate challenge was therefore a process involving both cultures. Regarding the organization culture the first step was to avoid any new employees becoming indoctrinated in the existing culture, while separately creating an awareness of exactly what the culture was to existing staff and how it was detrimental to the future of the organization. With regard to both family and organization cultures the second step was to identify the components of the old cultures, try to influence and change them, then move to changing the cultures.

Immersion in cultural intervention

Traditional wisdom is that beliefs and values influence behaviour, which in turn influences beliefs and values. But culture was a liability when the shared beliefs and values were not in keeping with the needs or intentions of the organization. Blumenthal and Haspeslagh (1994) wrote that to qualify as corporate transformation a majority of individuals in an organization had to change their behaviours. They offered three types of transformation. First, a *quantum improvement in operations* achieved through re-engineering business processes, restructured roles and responsibilities, redefinition of performance standards and measurements, which would become manifest through reduced costs and improved quality, efficiency and service. Second, a *strategic transformation* achieved through redefining business objectives, creating new competencies and harnessing those capabilities needed to meet market opportunities, which would become manifest through regaining a sustainable competitive advantage. Third, a *corporate self-renewal* leading to the creation of the ability for the firm to anticipate and cope with change so that strategic and operational gaps did not develop going forward. Beer *et al.* (1990) had strongly argued that change accomplished through a changed organizational context would force new attitudes and behaviours on people. Therefore I needed to find a range of mechanisms to cause an ultimate change in culture.

Beginning mid-1994 I commenced implementing the following initiatives.

- *Changed people*: to recruit new personnel and transfer those with the desired new characteristics to key or influential roles.
- *Changed places*: to move aside those who resisted change while seeking to move different people with different experiences and prior learning into key positions.
- *Changed structures, systems and technologies*: rewards were introduced and appraisal, monitoring, budgeting and control systems were linked to specific required behaviour. The organization structure was slowly reformed into a professional, team-based structure.
- *Changed beliefs, attitudes and behaviour*: to create an environment to change beliefs, values and attitudes through formal and/or informal re-education of those receptive to change and also through the creation of pockets of commitment through the use of role models for the desired attitudes and behaviour.
- A series of formal one-on-one counselling meetings were held where detailed changes were outlined as they related to each individual by defining what was expected of each person in the 'new' organization. I asked for and expected new ideas. At subsequent management meetings each individual was asked to forward one new idea per meeting on how to improve operational efficiency which would then be discussed and suggestions offered. But responsibility would then revert to the proposer of the idea to see it through and to report on measurable progress.
- *Change and development of a new corporate image*: this progressed through formal communication, through advertising and promotional campaigns, by physical redecoration of office buildings and office environments, by talking and by creating a mental change awareness and an expectation of change.
- *Changed strategy*: by encouraging managers to identify and clarify the future, also through identification of the degree of imbalance between where the firm was and where it needed to be, the need for change was

revealed. Change strategies arose initially through experimentation and probing strategies rather than strategies imposed from the top down. As management was not experienced in strategy formulation I resolved to commence this through learning curves where small initiatives were encouraged and experimented with. As an example, while preparing for ISO 9000 a review of internal work practices revealed significant shortcomings. Middle managers were empowered to identify best practices and to experiment with changed procedures to come up with improved methods. The result was a series of experiments where several procedures were tried and rejected, but each successive experiment was an improvement on the previous one.

• Additionally the confidence, commitment and team-building which emerged through the process added to the benefits of the exercise. My task was to ensure that the desired futures of the individuals fell within my future strategic intentions.

Results of the change process

The various actions undertaken to change the organization culture succeeded in bringing it to a state of transition. Actions had included constant communication, improvement in operations, business re-engineering, restructured roles and responsibilities, redefinition of performance standards and new staff recruitment.

Outcomes included the reunification as a whole of the various organization fragments that had broken apart several years earlier; the withdrawal of the founder from operational involvement and his removal as a person of last appeal to the organization; the relocation of one of my brothers to manage a branch depot; the emergence of my second brother as a better manager; the turnaround in overall financial performance; the building of pockets of commitment particularly within new additions to the firm; the reduction in the number of problems and disputes that otherwise used to arise in day-to-day business activities.

Through this process it had been important to generate a high level of discomfort with the culture as it was before the change in order to make it less likely that individuals would seek to return to the earlier state. This was achieved through constant referral to the crisis that the organization had encountered and the near-fatal outcome, and also that the cultural and other conditions which caused the crisis could re-emerge if conscious efforts were not undertaken to ensure their removal.

A new style of management helped to move towards this permanent change. Individuals liked being empowered to experiment, to question and to change things as evidenced by their requests for more autonomy, more freedom and permission to experiment in areas not included within original briefs. They welcomed the responsibility of being held accountable as it involved a transfer of authority and responsibility to them. They appreciated the involvement in debate and communication, of being listened to and having their opinions taken on board. They enjoyed being able to make decisions that would not be overridden. Those who previously had held little responsibility were encouraged to take it.

Another outcome was that directors who had previously been powerful and unquestioned figures lost some of this power to a new style of management where the exercise of power, for power's sake, was not welcome. Middle managers, previously meek and obedient, now challenged directives where they believed that there might be a better way. The organization moved to a healthy, open and enquiring environment where the desire to learn began to supplant the desire to simply perform as instructed. Ultimately, in 1997, one of my brothers resigned and set up as a competitor.

Phase II: immersion – reflections and lessons

Through the process I learned, within family businesses, that communication occurs least when it is needed most. Positions become entrenched and drenched in emotion and I believe it is this failure to communicate which leads to the high failure rate of second generation family businesses. Family and individual values, and often stubborn pride, erodes the rational decision-making process. In an environment where family owners of a business exert significant influence it is proposed that this represented an extra environmental force requiring the same level of awareness, management action and strategy development as was warranted by any other environmental force. The determinants of culture within the organization include the family, which is a significant influence both inside and outside the organization.

Through the culture change process I learned many things. For example while organization culture referred to common beliefs, attitudes and values it was the beliefs, attitudes and values that *individuals* possessed that had to be changed if culture itself was to change. Within the business, culture was both an input and an output, as senior managers were as much a product of the culture as they were creators of it. Therefore successful change had to be led from within, in particular by me as CEO. Culture change could certainly not have commenced without clear leadership, consistent energy and commitment from the top. Also the time-scale to achieve a culture change was not as short as had originally been anticipated. Far from being achieved in a year, I discovered that a total time-scale of two to three years was necessary to change culture to that needed to make the organization vibrant and forward looking.

I learned that no single change strategy on its own appeared capable of transforming the organization as all single strategies would ultimately interlink and have tangible and intangible connections to other areas of the organization. Each of these linkages and the degrees of impact would have to be identified, anticipated and planned if consolidation and then transformation was to be achieved. To achieve this I would have to continue to learn about and deeply understand the organization. I learned that culture change is costly in time, effort, emotions and in the strains on relationships that arise as roles are changed, long-standing members bypassed and power groups broken apart. In my case this was compounded by the fact that it was a family organization.

Yet I knew that some, much less all, of these types of changes would not be achieved over time without running into various types and levels of resistance. Like every other aspect of the organization, resistance would be capable of being managed once the sources and levels were understood. However, in my particular case the family resistance could have been lessened if the founder had clearly communicated from the beginning the matters which were communicated too late. Finally I learned that an alternative course of action such as splitting the business is an alternative where sibling rivalry becomes so intense as to threaten the business itself.

References

Baden-Fuller, C. and Stopford, J. M. (1992) *Rejuvenating the Mature Business: The Competitive Challenge.* Routledge, London.

Beer, M., Eisenstat, R. A., and Spector, B. (1990) Why Change Programmes Don't Produce Change, *Harvard Business Review*, November–December: 158–166.

Blumenthal, B. and Haspeslagh, P. (1994) Towards a Definition of Corporate Transformation, *Sloan Management Review*, Spring: 101–106.

Dunphy, D. C. and Stace, D. A. (1988) Transformational and Coercive Strategies for Planned Organizational Change: Beyond the OD Model, *Organizational Studies*, 9(3): 317–334.

Dunphy, D. C. and Stace, D. A. (1992) Transitions, Turnarounds and Transformations: Alternative Paths in Strategic Change. Paper delivered to the Strategic Management Society Conference, London.

Gabarro, J. J. (1985) When a New Manager Takes Charge, *Harvard Business Review*, May–June: 110–123.

Gabarro, J. J. (1987) *The Dynamics of Taking Charge.* Harvard Business School Press, Boston, MA.

Johnson, G. (1987) *Strategic Change and the Management Process.* Blackwell, Oxford.

Romanelli, E. and Tushman, M. L. (1994) Organizational Transformation as Punctuated Equilibrium: An Empirical Test, *Academy of Management Journal*, 37: 1141–1166.

Schein, E. (1983) Corporate Culture: What is It and How to Change It', invited address to Society of Sloan Fellows.

Sheldon, A. (1980) Organizational Paradigms: A Theory of Organizational Change, *Organizational Dynamics*, 8(3): 61–80.

Smyth, P. and Leach, P. (1993) *The Simpson Xavier Guide to the Family Business in Ireland*. Blackwater Press, Dublin.

Williams, A., Dobson, P. and Walters, J. (1993) *Changing Culture: New Organizational Approaches*. Institute of Personnel Management, London.

Chapter 4

Whose life is it anyway?

Managing the psychological contract

Ann Parkinson

Context

> The organization has some responsibility to me – there is a psychological
> contract, which says my value to you is more than the fulfilment of a
> function, I would look to the organization to do whatever it is reasonable
> to do within its powers to assist in the development of my career – the
> development lies with me.

Objectives

This chapter tells the story of a research project and its practical applications
born out of working for part of the United Kingdom division of a multinational organization in the high-tech sector which for the purposes of this
chapter will be known as AnyCo Inc. I will be introducing a number of
characters and issues that could be at large in any organization and illus-
trating how the issues raised impacted on AnyCo. The key issues addressed in
this chapter are those of retention of key skills and career expectations,
particularly of 'knowledge workers' who are most likely to be the subject of
what is frequently referred as the Talent Wars. However, the lessons from the
research reach further than AnyCo and I hope will resonate with your own
experience as both an employee and a manager. This research gave insights
into the importance of the line manager in shaping expectations and
providing the key to managing the organization's relationship with its
employees. Highlighting the issues of a consistent approach to such issues as
communication and management development, the chapter will explore in
particular the opportunities for developing the relationship between
individuals and their managers through HR practices of career development,
performance management, mentoring and coaching.

Setting the context

I was working with my colleagues in a recently established division of AnyCo
that had been started as a new venture some five years earlier, bringing a new

area of skills and expertise to a company that had traditionally 'grown its own' within the context of a strong culture. This is the story of many of those who had joined this division from both within and outside AnyCo, and out of their narratives a model of their understanding of the unwritten contract and expectations of their organization emerged that provides a perspective on the employment relationship and managing people in a large organization.

AnyCo is organized geographically so that AnyCo(UK) is part of the European division but subject to demands from the parent company in the United States. While successful in the United Kingdom at the time of the research, the rest of European sales lagged considerably which counterbalanced the achievements and left the United Kingdom subject to financial and headcount constraints, especially as the new CEO wanted to make an early impact on performance which at that time was measured by the bottom line.

AnyCo, like many other organizations, underwent dramatic change in the 1990s, driven by various competitive, economic, technological and social pressures which forced restructuring and downsizing. In rebuilding the organization, AnyCo developed different forms of employment by creating a virtual workforce from other organizations in peripheral activities, to introducing fixed term contracts for new graduates, as well retaining the traditional permanent contract for those with 'core' skills (Figure 4.1). As well as short-term contractors, part-timers and agency staff, it had also been developing strategic partnerships with its natural competitors, which had taken it well beyond the core–peripheral models first identified in the 1980s (Atkinson, 1985; Handy, 1985).

In common with many others in this industry, AnyCo was renowned for excellent job-related skills training, but when promoting skilled people into managerial roles had focused on the legal aspects of their role rather than training them in managing people. This lack of development began to be

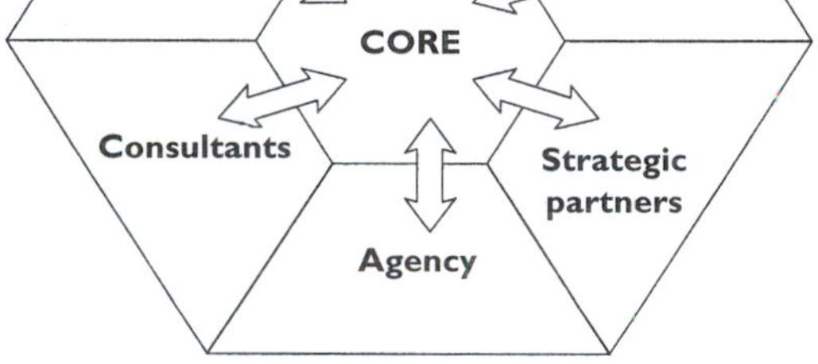

Expanded core–periphery model

Figure 4.1 Creating a virtual peripheral workforce (after Kildare, 1996).

apparent as the personnel department had been transformed into HR with a service unit looking after the formal aspects of pay and conditions, and providing HR consultancy services when requested through a single adviser supporting more than one division on all other aspects. Managers in the organization, and many of those joining, had been brought up with traditional models of personnel managing the processes of recruitment, training and development, and performance appraisal for them. They saw people management as an additional task to add to an already busy role which came lower down their priority list, especially as it was one for which they had not been prepared.

The new division had brought in a number of experienced people with the new skills it needed to work alongside those who had survived the organization restructuring five years earlier. This had created the unusual situation of a large influx of people later into their careers, who had differing expectations into what was recognized as a strong culture. Over the years AnyCo had developed its own traditions and norms which it had not occurred to anyone that this new intake might need to know. A good illustration of one of these unwritten norms lay at the heart of the issue that the research project sought to understand: in the AnyCo culture it was seen as usual to raise the subject of your next career move with your line manager and that was how people had traditionally moved on.

'Line managers are not equipped to be alert to the alarm signals'

The research was instigated as part of the process of reviewing the relationship it had with its employees, using career management as the tool to both understand and manage expectations. AnyCo had recognized that in the old culture people had sat back and allowed the company to manage their careers for them; the period following restructuring had forced them onto their own resources totally unprepared, and now they wanted to achieve a balance somewhere between the two. As an employer of highly marketable 'knowledge workers', they also wanted to retain their specialist skill base and had the very real operational problem of an unexpectedly high turnover. Managers were finding that key members of staff would present their resignation unanticipated, leaving the company for a competitor when there was a similar role available in AnyCo that they could have been managed into, had the manager been aware that the individual was ready for a career move. Many of those leaving were those who had been recruited when the division had been established some four or five years previously: 'the only time people don't register they want a move is when they are talking to someone else outside' (AnyCo manager).

AnyCo wanted to understand the career expectations that people now had, given the changes in employment and the market since the upheaval of the early 1990s. They also wanted to explore how they could have anticipated that someone was ready for a career move before they approached their competitors, only learning about it at resignation by which time the individual had already committed themselves to leave. Practically they also wanted to identify the possibilities for the process needed to support career development work and to identify implications for the role of the manager.

The project had started with running a series of career management workshops for managers to familiarize them with the concepts that we would then be using with their skilled, professional workforce. The research project itself took place after many of the managers had experienced the programme and had started to think about their career, often for the first time. A sample of them, along with individuals from their teams, were chosen and willing to be interviewed in depth to provide a representative sample from across the division. These conversations were focused around their perceptions of their careers based on Schein's career anchors as well as examining their views of the relationship they had with AnyCo.

The general outcomes of these conversations or interviews were fed back to AnyCo, both at an early stage in the form of a report and discussion panel, and much later after becoming the main database of my doctoral research, from which the following narratives and theories emerged. It was from this that we were able to develop both answers for AnyCo and to begin to explain what was going on for use in other organizations facing similar issues. These in-depth interviews and the analysis that followed showed that there were many differences between how people viewed their career and their relationship with AnyCo, but within those differences there were commonalities which allowed me to identify four or five distinctive general types of people working in the organization, irrespective of level, gender or performance, who are introduced below in the following sections. My subsequent presentations and discussion with other companies and practitioners suggest that these 'types' are just as likely to be working in other organizations as well.

Kim and Jo, and Sam and Alex

Kim's story – 'I come to work to earn money'

'I was going to have a brand new BMW by the time I was 21 and be a millionaire when I am 35,' Kim remembered starting out on the career journey with no goals, not having a clue what to do, but no doubts that wanting to earn money was the prime driver. After university the choice of job was driven more by money than other considerations: 'First job? That was remuneration, I would have done just about anything anywhere. I wanted to make as much money as fast as possible'. The job had come easily too, falling into it just like most of the other moves, 'very little at my instigation, usually somebody else's'.

After a brilliant start with the next job including an attractive salary and a company car, 'they kept paying me more and more money', Kim found it difficult to make radical moves, 'I couldn't afford to take whatever pay drop that would come' and saw any career progression just in terms of earning more money. Getting married made Kim consider the security, pension and the other benefits as well, recognizing that moving jobs would lose the total package, part of which was working for a well-known company. Eventually the ambition to be a millionaire was rationalized, 'the key is whether you want to be a multimillionaire or whether you want to live the lifestyle of a millionaire – if I won the lottery I wouldn't work, I work because I need to, not because that is my life'.

Kim wasn't a great one for career planning, happy to 'tootle along' in the job while it was enjoyable, preferring to wait for the next thing to happen or for someone to make contact, 'I suppose everyone has their own way of managing their moves and their lives, I'd rather just keep my options open really'. Most of the time, job moves had come from other people making suggestions, particularly one or two good managers, who had also helped in making decisions which now also needed the family taking into consideration. Making changes hadn't been easy: last time Kim had found the move a bit of a culture shock, feeling nervous to start with, which might have been worry at the prospect of failure, however within a few months everything fell into place, although it had been painful at the time.

Jo's story – 'It's not broke'

'I like doing a job well and being seen to be good'. Jo had recognized that achievement was important, wanting to be able to point to something and say, 'Yes I am a success', working for the most successful company in the industry was a part of that and no mean feat for someone who did not start out with particular career goals.

'Of course people nowadays don't see the organization I did, ten years ago it was very different, people were almost certain of job security, life was a little more leisurely, now if they are committed to doing well, they need to do things outside of their normal day-to-day job to be seen to be a contributor – now it's a case of if you commit to me, I will commit to you having a career', it didn't seem so very different from the traditional 'you give your all to the company and the company gives back'. With every expectation of still doing the job in five years' time, although recognizing that in this day and age nothing was certain, Jo could see that those with shorter tenure didn't look any further forward than the job they were doing now, to which they were committed but often not to the same extent as the 'older hands'.

Looking back, all the career moves so far had come as a result of feeling either things were not working out or through not being able to achieve, 'that time when I had absolutely nothing to do and I had a lot of experience and skills and needed to be involved in something. I was just keen to get another job and out of what I was doing, desperate would probably be a better word, but it did make me question more clearly what I was going to be doing in a job, as opposed to looking at where it might lead in the future', Jo thought back, 'the other times were when the job had become boring and approaches had come at the right time'. These changes had been enjoyable, especially the riskier moves, 'it fell into place, so I was quite excited about that, and then finding I loved it, it was really good fun'. Jo firmly believes that the organization should take some responsibility for managing people's careers, 'they are huge assets, they cost huge amounts, so the organization should be deploying its people to best advantage, moving those which are in the wrong job'. When head-hunters call, Jo usually thinks, 'Does the company value me? Is someone still thinking about me?' before politely ending the conversation and putting the phone down.

The area that Kim and Jo seemed to have in common was that they have both taken a somewhat passive role in managing their careers either making moves in response to negative situations or at others' bidding. In Jo's case 'I've generally done things because people have asked me to do them', or being influenced by other people particularly managers in the organization for Kim although previous choices had been influenced by parents or teachers, 'my father worked for AnyCo', 'my father was a frustrated engineer'. This had started early on when several had reported that they had 'just drifted into' their career and equally they expected the organization to provide them with opportunities as they are sometimes quite nervous about making changes but also may not have the confidence to negotiate for themselves.

Sam's story – 'A desire to get on'

'Did I really want to be a successful pop star?', Sam laughed when thinking about starting out on a varied career, 'I still want to make that difference and do something important, and I certainly value the recognition, being well thought of and having the respect of others, so perhaps not much has changed'. Sam had always been ambitious, needing stimulation and challenge which had been the driving force behind any career changes. Once the challenge had gone, if nothing was in the offing, there had always seemed to be the opportunity to create a new one. 'I'm not interested in just keeping things as they are', others may have expected the organization to do it all for them, to provide their career ladder, but Sam was always ready to initiate change and enjoyed doing it, that would even extend to leaving if necessary. However, this didn't mean giving up easily as Sam had found failure very tough and stressful.

As a strategy for ensuring that there would always be career opportunities, Sam had added the practical management degree to provide a broader base and an insurance policy. Looking back this seemed to be part of an overall strategy to remain in control of life and career decisions, as was considering what was needed to get on, 'How good am I at reading the situation and responding? Is part of getting on how comfortable one is about being able to play the politics?'

Being in control was not just in terms of progressing and wanting to run a business unit, Sam wanted to be able to get the balance right with career and a personal life, recognizing there seemed to be lot of confusion on what was now acceptable: 'If I'm 30 something with a [spouse] and two children, how ambitious am I supposed to be these days? Could one expect organizations to provide security and stability any more, especially for those with children? For me the family may be the key influence, but I guess my career dominates, but I think there's a responsibility that the organization does have, not putting people in the position of having to choose.'

Alex's story – 'I know what I'm talking about'

There hadn't been a time when Alex couldn't remember being interested in technical things, which had led to studying computing at university, and from then onto the technical grounding that had been at the core of the career. Most moves had had the need to keep those skills marketable and taking opportunities to fill in the gaps was a priority over which company those were gained in. Thinking back, Alex reflected, 'I would still recommend that if someone was going to go into computing that they get a really good technical grounding, you can always move out of it if you are good enough but there are always jobs for programmers and system administrators.'

There had been times in the past when Alex had felt exposed, coming into a new area, there was every possibility of being faced with not knowing the technology. Until the situation had become familiar and it was possible to have a technical conversation about it, that feeling of nervousness and discomfort had not been dispelled. 'It's interesting how you don't always take your own good advice', Alex mused, 'I really want to avoid technical obsolescence, so if I need to I'll start to do some work on my own to build my technical skills up again.' It was a dilemma, the management job had seemed a good move at the time, not wanting to be 100 per cent technical, and particularly with the previous company being restructured and then sold around you. There really was a kick from seeing the end result achieved through somebody else and managing the operation, but not the thought of getting involved in the more 'psychological' aspects of managing people – who needs to know about transactional analysis and that sort of thing, it certainly wasn't the kind of thing to be assessed on.

Coming late into this organization meant it was difficult to see where the next career move would be. Many people, secure in their skill base, only looked to get two maybe three years out of the company and then move on to the next to gain more skills, not believing this culture where it seemed okay to say you wanted a new job. 'Then again I have always had some idea that I would like my own business some day, so perhaps . . .'

Sam and Alex seemed to be more active in their careers however, wanting to be more in control of them. Their career moves were made positively taking into consideration building skills and their self-development. For Sam control of career meant seeking out new challenges and partly working to achieve a balanced lifestyle, 'what level of personal commitment am I willing to trade for that move', while for Alex developing expertise was critical to self-image and being able to be self-reliant, 'I like being the specialist, you need the expertise for confidence'. They both felt that the individual was responsible for maintaining their employability, this was partly because both had been victims of redundancy or organizational reorganization which meant loss of trust in organizations for Alex. Early on in their careers they were clearer about what they wanted 'I have always had a pretty clear idea of what I wanted to do and where I wanted to be.'

The other dimension that became apparent was that of what type of relationship they each wanted from AnyCo. Kim and Alex seemed to share the wish for a more formal business relationship with AnyCo with the focus on security and 'monetizable' rewards from the organization where they were offering skills in return for delivery, and as managers they were expecting to manage the task. Whereas Jo and Sam were looking for more from their relationship with AnyCo, wanting respect and recognition in return for offering their commitment and 'whole self', and as managers they expect to manage people in delivering the task. These dimensions of career 'directedness' and the type of relationship they were looking for in AnyCo seemed to be the key factors that drove their expectations of their organization and career, which is summarized in Figure 4.2 and will be explained in a little more depth later. Each of the characters I have described above were based on a composite of those participants in the research who clearly contributed to a particular type, and uses their words; however, there were those who had characteristics of more than one type showing that the model is potentially more complex. It was not possible to anticipate into which character type an individual would fall from gender, level or role in the organization, suggesting that in every work team, as stated earlier, there is likely to be a mix.

> They all have different expectations – I can't generalise – many want to get on, but understand it differently, driven by peer pressure, family pressures – lots of external things drive people.
>
> (AnyCo manager)

The last 'type' that the research project uncovered was developed from the perceptions of the managers when they were clearly wearing their 'managerial' hats.

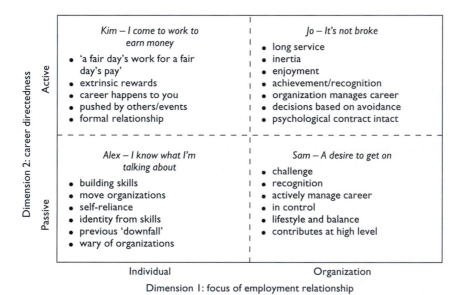

Figure 4.2 Expectations of the employment relationship (adapted from Parkinson, 1999a).
© Ann Parkinson, 2003.

Gerry's story – 'Building the relationship'

'Although I have always known people were individuals, with different sets of expectations, as an organization, perhaps we manage them as if they had the same career goals. We consider that people see their career as progression of both responsibility and self importance in getting to a certain status position. One colleague had described the career as a series of mountain climbs where you go up and then you plateau and then you go up once more.' However, since becoming a manager, Gerry had found it more difficult to see the mechanisms to progress one's own career in those same terms, and had recognized that some of the most enjoyable times had been when in a learning environment, growing with the organization. In the future it would be more likely the career would be finding opportunities to fill in gaps in experience.

Gerry agreed that people should make some investment to move whichever way the organization's requirement went, but also recognized that many of them struggled with what that entailed. As a manager there was still a guidance role, helping people progress in the organization, Gerry realized there was more to it, the manager could encourage, support and coach but the organization had a responsibility to ensure the opportunities were there for people to succeed in a job, to build up skills, to progress and to be proud of the organization. This was beyond the legal responsibilities of things like health and safety. 'I am now expected to be responsible for the career development for the people who work for me, coach them, mentoring and things like that as well, I am sure there are people better qualified than I am. I have to cope with any of the issues that my people may have.'

'The organization needs me to have a good relationship with my people,' Gerry reflected, 'as they often don't want or have the opportunity to be involved at a higher level with the organization. And anyway working all over the place, like we do today, with people not having set desks, I am happy for people to work from home; which means I have to go by whether I feel they're doing all the things they should be doing, and those I feel less comfortable about, I check up on. I spend quite a bit of time going to see my scattered group, rather than getting them to come to me.' How could you tell how well that relationship was working? Gerry pondered, 'Of course there are things like recognition events to show how well you thought of people and the annual get-togethers such as the Christmas dinner to build the team. I suppose really the main opportunity to gauge the effectiveness of how well that relationship was working was in the annual appraisal round and as someone had put it, how the level of compensation compared with expectation.'

Gerry's tale illustrates the manager's view of the relationship and brings to the fore the key role in managing the relationship with employees. Not only did Gerry express the realization that in organizations we all tend to treat employees as if they all had the same expectations and were motivated by the same things, but also that paradoxically we know that everyone is different. The key issue that starts to emerge from Gerry is that of how little preparation many line managers have been given to take over what in effect has traditionally been seen as personnel roles. AnyCo, like many other organizations, had reorganized personnel into an HR model with central services looking after the formal aspect of the employment contract such as pay and conditions, and advisers to divisions to support them in all other aspects, without training or development for those divisions or their managers in taking on the more formal aspects of managing people such as recruitment, managing the appraisal process and development. What the research revealed in summary was that there are a number of different sets of expectations or psychological contracts operating in a group at any time which the manager has had take over the role of HR in managing as the deliverer of HR practices to them.

> I don't look at AnyCo as a big organization, really to me AnyCo is your manager and your manager's manager.

The second major issue the research raised was that of what emerged as the difference between the formal contract

> the contract that AnyCo has with its employees in a deliverable sense, they're from AnyCo rather than from your manager . . . anything I guess human resources get involved with, you know, car, insurance, pensions . . . as a manager I've got absolutely no influence whatsoever

and the informal contract relating to the psychological contract

> broadening your skills, experience, representing AnyCo at conferences, things like that which build people's skills and competencies, which are by no means contractual.

Again the key actor in managing the informal contract is the line manager as shown in Figure 4.3.

What was AnyCo's side of the contract?

One interesting aspect that was revealed by the research analysis was how differently people viewed what AnyCo expected of them, although they were all working for the same division with the same formal, legal contract.

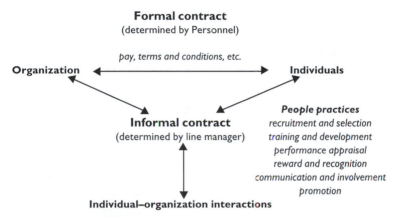

Figure 4.3 Aspects of the employment relationship (Parkinson, 1999b).
© Ann Parkinson, 2003.

These differing views were driven by each character's own requirements, reinforcing that how we see the organization we work for is subjective, as demonstrated by Box 4.1.

What was going on in AnyCo(UK)? Frameworks for understanding

For those interested in understanding what was happening in AnyCo, there are several areas of theory and previous research that can help explain what was going on. These will allow us to judge the extent to which the models above are relevant for other organizations and to understand their implications.

Explaining the character types

There are several areas of theory that help explain how the main character types have come about of which I am going to touch on the half-dozen that seem to have the most to offer in providing a framework for understanding. Earlier I suggested there were two main dimensions behind how people saw their employment relationship which drive the typologies I have described.

The first dimension, the type of contract sought, can be understood in terms of organizational commitment and more recently as the psychological contract. Organizational commitment had its roots mainly in the 1970s and 1980s from the focus on excellence and new models of personnel management such as the rise of the Human Resources school (Cox and Parkinson, 2002). Organizational commitment was seen to have three main aspects and has been defined as:

Who	Individual's needs and expectations	Organization's needs and expectations

Jo
It's not broke
	• company manages career
	• provide opportunities for:
	  • enjoyment
	  • achievement
	  • fulfilment
	  • skills utilized
		• demonstrate commitment
		  to organization
		• doing the extra
		• contribution

Sam
A desire to
get on
	• challenge, being stretched
	• recognition
	• control over life, balance,
	  autonomy
	• guidance in career by company
		• significant contribution
		• loyalty
		• pound of flesh
		• managers represent
		  company

Alex *I know what I'm* *talking about*	• build skills • able to utilize specialist skills • a stepping stone to next job	• demonstrate commitment to job • provide specialist skills

Kim
I come to work
to earn money
	• money, extrinsic rewards
	• security
	• career moves 'happen'
	• written contract
	  • four weeks' notice
	  • salary
	  • health and safety
		• business relationship
		• delivery of results

Gerry
Building the
relationship
	• advancement
	• responsibility
	• written contract terms
	• opportunity to use and build
	  skills
	• career development
		• high work ethic
		• doing the things they ought
		• manage own careers
		• managers to deliver
		  to professionals

Box 4.1 Summary of individual views of what the organization expects.

the relative strength of an individual's identification with and involvement in a particular organization. Conceptually, it can be characterized by at least three factors: (1) a strong belief in, and acceptance of the organization's goals and values, (2) a willingness to exert considerable effort on behalf of the organization, and (3) a strong desire to maintain membership in the organization.

(Porter *et al.*, 1974)

It is this 'relative strength of an individual's identification' which perhaps best describes that first dimension in Figure 4.2.

Following the major restructuring and downsizing of the late 1980s and early 1990s another aspect was highlighted in the form of the psychological contract which had been first identified some thirty years earlier and described by Schein (1978):

> the actual terms remain implicit; they are not written down anywhere. But the mutual expectations formed between the employee and the employer function like a contract in that if either party fails to meet the expectations, serious consequences will follow – demotivation, turnover, lack of advancement, or termination.
>
> (Schein, 1978)

Schein describes the psychological contract as a process that is 'interactive, unfolding through mutual influence and mutual bargaining' (Schein, 1980) and Herriot and Pemberton (1996) illustrate this through their process model, Figure 4.4, which demonstrates that it is a dynamic process that changes over time as both sides in the contract change their needs and what they can offer. The process also recognizes that when the offer changes, both sides have an opportunity to renegotiate their contract or leave.

The AnyCo research found that the contract changing had an impact on how actively people pursued their career. Both Sam and Alex had been in situations where the organization's needs had changed, Sam had been able to stay in control of the situation and renegotiate, retaining commitment, whereas Alex had no control of the outcome and had been left wary of making a commitment to the next organization. This also illustrates an area of psychological contract theory that has looked at what triggers or events that define the contracting process where either side assesses or reassesses it. Schein (1978) suggests that events that symbolize mutual acceptance are related to everyday HR practices such as selection, performance appraisal, salary review and development, and are times when the employee and the

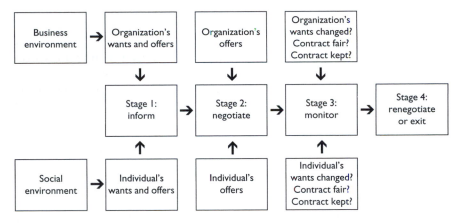

Figure 4.4 The four stages of psychological contracting (Herriot and Pemberton, 1996).

organization, usually represented by the line manager, have an exchange which can be seen as a negotiation or renegotiation as represented by Herriot and Pemberton's (1996) contracting process. Other writers see communication at the heart of determining how the psychological contract is viewed; Robinson and Rousseau (1994) found that managers who promote open two-way communication have the opportunity to resolve discrepancies in the psychological contract at an early stage.

> almost every piece of communication that you have, individual reviews, unit meetings, do you get a Christmas lunch? Some people for example are very sensitive about reviews, and it's almost like every communication you have with them relates back to the annual appraisal.
>
> (AnyCo manager)

Another view of the psychological contract looks at what happened in the aftermath of the early 1990s when what had often been seen to be a 'job for life' culture was decimated and long-standing psychological contracts were 'violated' as large numbers of people were unexpectedly made redundant. These violations can equally occur in a less dramatic way when expectations the individual may have about a job or their future in the organization are not realized. In AnyCo part of the retention problem occurred as new people's expectations about their careers, raised in the recruitment process when their initial psychological contract was formed, seemed to be disappointed as they were unaware of the culture that made this openly discussable unlike previous organizations. The key author in this area, Rousseau (1995), writes about the content of psychological contracts, 'individual beliefs, shaped by the organization, regarding terms of an exchange agreement between individuals and their organization', recognizing the differences between what she calls transactional contracts such as the one that Kim and Alex prefer in terms of a tangible transaction of pay in return for task performed within a specified time-scale. At the other extreme she describes the 'relational' contract as something more abstract and characterized by open ended relationships and investment from both sides such as Sam and Jo would rather have.

The other dimension of 'directedness' is informed by both career and other theories. It is worth observing that Schein (1978, 1980), Herriot and Pemberton (1996) and Rousseau (1995) all write about both psychological contract and careers, demonstrating that the two are interlinked. Brousseau et al. (1996) have developed a framework of career concepts that fits with our four characters in terms of transitional (Kim), linear (Jo), spiral (Sam) and expert (Alex) careers. The other key theory, that of Julian Rotter, who first described 'locus of control' in 1954 (McKenna, 1987) as a continuum of a dimension of personality, with those with an internal locus viewing control as related to their own efforts and talents, feeling confident that they can bring the changes needed in their environment. They are more likely to be seen as independent, achieving and dominant. At the other end, those with an external locus feel powerless to bring about change, controlled by forces outside their control, chance, fate, other people. One group of researchers demonstrated that the internal locus of control correlated positively with the quality of the management relationship (Kinicki and Vecchio, 1994).

Role of line management in the psychological contract

> the bit where the rubber hits the road is actually the first line manager.
>
> (AnyCo manager)

An area that had been missing, particularly in the psychological contract literature, was the role of the line manager in the psychological contract. Rousseau and others suggest that the nature of the relationship the individual has with the organization is shaped by HR practices but have failed to recognize that these are now delivered by line management in many organizations. The most relevant seems to be 'leader member exchange' theory, which reinforces the importance of the quality of the relationship between the individual and their manager: 'high-quality exchanges are consistently related to favourable individual outcomes . . . we view the relationship with one's supervisor as a lens through which the entire work relationship is viewed' (Gertstner and Day, 1997). It was the importance of the line manager that was perhaps the most significant insight to come out of the research and that influenced both my own and AnyCo's next steps. This seems a case of a 'flash of the blindingly obvious' but often difficult to see when involved directly in the issue.

So what? – implications for AnyCo and beyond

Following the research we developed a career management process within the division that recognized the key role that the manager had in influencing careers. All managers completed the original two-day course, which was now seen more as part of their own development, particularly in understanding individual differences and different career orientations so that they could begin to support their own staff. Having recognized that it was likely that at any one time only up to a quarter of staff may be ready for a career move, it was decided a version of the course would be offered optionally to 'professionals' when it was felt they would be ready to benefit from it, as their line managers would now be in a better position to gauge this. Career management was tied more firmly into the personal development process through developing staff being included in managers' objectives, and in recognition that not everyone found it easy to talk to their immediate manager provision was made for the second line manager to take on the career management role when appropriate. Finally a panel consisting of a manager from each department as well as the HR adviser, the career development forum, was established to focus on career issues, reviewing individuals' progress and to facilitate moves within AnyCo to avoid managers holding back key people, with the risk of losing those skills to competitors. In the longer term AnyCo recognized the need to develop their managers' skills and have embarked on a partnership with a leading business school to put their managers through the MBA programme.

The wider implications for organizations of the different characters are in understanding employees' differing needs which may not be confined to the more obvious stereotypes and issues such as how they react to change, management style or what aid they need in managing their career in the organization are likely to be different. When major changes are planned, organizations need to take into account the potential impact on different views of the relationship for each group and how to manage them. Also apparent for this group of 'knowledge workers' was their need to balance work and home, their need for challenge, and their need to be stretched. By understanding their career aspirations, their managers and mentors can help the organization know whether it should be buying in or training new skills, developing future management talent or renegotiating the informal contract to enable a lifestyle requirement to be met. Where these are talents that the organization wants to retain understanding these needs can be invaluable.

In order to take into account individual needs and expectations, a different approach may be required to the relationship with them through their manager, who emerges as the central player in the informal relationship between the organization and the employee. A good relationship may mitigate against harmful effects brought about by external forces, also it is how managers model the values of the organization that will determine whether the individual feels they identify with the organization and want to stay. The organization also needs to recognize that the line manager is likely to be managing as many different types of contract as members of the team, as well as managing their own contract with their boss and the potential tensions that this may bring, especially when there are potential conflicting objectives.

The delegation of traditional HR practices to line management underlines the crucial need for organizations to train and develop their managers to meet their increased responsibility, especially where they are the interface with specialist skills. Not only do they need to be prepared for managing HR issues such as appraisal, communication and assessing training and development needs for individuals, but they increasingly need to understand individual differences, in the context of developing their interpersonal skills. This may take many of them on into the domain of a coaching, mentoring role and working with those who require guidance in managing their career. The other issue for HR practitioners is the need for consistency in how managers deal with their teams as they are seen as the embodiment of the organization, underpinned by the consistent messages to employees from that consistent approach. It is also incumbent on HR practitioners to ensure that those relationship-building opportunities such as in communication, recruitment and selection, performance management, and training and development are supported and

> will require a fundamental rethink of HRM policies, the end to many unitary assumptions, a re-education process for line managers and employees alike, a call for leadership and not just facilitation from HR professionals.
>
> (Sparrow, 1996)

And finally . . .

Having spent much of my own career as a practitioner in a large organization, it was easy to be involved in issues, but not to have the opportunity to stand back and understand 'what was going on'. I found that I was better able to take a more objective view and able to see the problem that needed to be addressed before working with my staff to develop solutions. However, it was only with the opportunity to be immersed in research and apply theory that I was able to come to an understanding of the different perspectives and the issues raised for AnyCo, and have now embarked on extending this research into other companies. I hope in telling their stories that my five characters have been able to convey enough of that understanding to provide practical ideas or to encourage others into their own voyages of discovery.

> What we call the beginning is often the end
> And to make an end is to make a beginning.
> The end is where we start from.
> (T. S. Eliot, *Four Quartets*, 1943)

References

Atkinson, J. (1985) The Changing Corporation, in D. Clutterbuck (ed.) *New Patterns of Work*. Gower, Aldershot.

Brousseau, K. R., Driver, M. J., Eneroth, K. and Larsson, R. (1996) Career Pandemonium: Realigning Organizations and Individuals, *Academy of Management Executive, Special Issue: Careers in the 21st Century*, 10(4): 52–67.

Cox, P. and Parkinson, A. (2002) Values and the Employment Relationship, in G. Hollinshead, P. Nicholls and S. Tailby (eds) *Employee Relations*, 2nd edition. FT Prentice Hall, London.

Gertstner, C. R. and Day, D. V. (1997) Meta-Analysis Review of Leader-Member Exchange Theory: Correlates and Construct Issues, *Journal of Applied Psychology*, 82(6): 827–844.

Handy, C. (1985) *The Future of Work: A Guide to Changing Society*. Blackwell, Oxford.

Herriot, P. and Pemberton, C. (1996) Contracting Careers, *Human Relations*, 49(6): 757–791.

Kildare, G. (1996) Presentation to Future Work Forum, Henley Management College, Brunel University, UK.

Kinicki, A. J. and Vecchio, R. P. (1994) Influences on the Quality of Supervisor–Subordinate Relations: The Role of Time-Pressure, Organization Commitment, and Locus of Control, *Journal of Organizational Behaviour*, 15: 75–82.

McKenna, E. F. (1987) *Psychology in Business: Theory and Applications*. Lawrence Erlbaum, Hove, East Sussex, UK.

Parkinson, A. (1999a) Sustaining Constructive Relationships across Cultural Boundaries, in P. Joynt and R. Morton (eds) *The Global HR Manager*. IPD Books, London.

Parkinson, A. (1999b) The Changing Nature of the Employment Relationship: Mapping the Subjective Terrain of the Psychological Contract. Unpublished doctoral thesis, Henley Management College, Brunel University, UK.

Porter, L. W., Steers, R. M., Mowday, R. T. and Boulian, P. V. (1974) Organizational Commitment, Job Satisfaction and Turnover among Psychiatric Technicians, *Journal of Applied Psychology*, 59: 603–609.

Robinson, S. L. and Rousseau, D. M. (1994) Violating the Psychological Contract: Not the Exception but the Norm, *Journal of Organizational Behaviour*, 15: 245–259.

Rousseau, D. M. (1995) *Psychological Contracts in Organizations: Understanding Written and Unwritten Agreements*. Sage, Thousand Oaks, CA.

Schein, E. H. (1978) *Career Dynamics: Matching Individual and Organizational Needs*. Addison-Wesley, Reading, MA.

Schein, E. H. (1980) *Organizational Psychology*, 3rd edn. Prentice Hall, Englewood Cliffs, NJ.

Sparrow, P. R. (1996) Transitions in the Psychological Contract: Some Evidence from the Banking Sector, *Human Resource Management Journal*, 4: 75–92.

Chapter 5

A manager's model for assessing and understanding 360-degree survey feedback effects on teams

William J. Kohley

In the industrial workplace, teamwork is essential to productivity – management is well aware of this fact. To realize productivity through teamwork, management has tinkered with ingenious ways to provide teams with 'input' on how well they are 'working together' with other teams. This is considered 'inter-team' feedback. Managers can use these inter-team feedback systems as a means for productivity 'improvement' programmes. Academics and consultants have researched feedback systems and suggest they can moderate behaviour across organizational systems. Managers are anxious to leverage survey feedback systems to meet performance objectives. Is the link as direct as 'provide feedback, increase productivity?' Some managers may think so. More than 70 per cent of organizations survey employees either annually or biannually (Paul and Bracken, 1995). Why? Because peer group (team) feedback has emerged as a significant information source for individuals and groups to moderate behaviour and increase efficiency. Good in theory, but is this what actually happens in the workplace? I put this question to test in the organization in which I work and what I learned about 360-degree survey feedback has significantly altered my approach to promoting change through inter-team communication. I strongly suggest leaders and managers to critically assess the use of survey feedback in their organizations.

Survey says . . .

At maximum, surveys give top management some data for changing practices or provide an index against which to compare trends (French and Bell, 1999). Most surveys are not used in an optimal way. At the organization in which I worked, this was true as well: you could hear employees grumbling about the process every quarter when the surveys were distributed. Poor use of survey-guided change tools are a concern because survey feedback processes continue to proliferate in modern-day organizations. Ask yourself, have you ever been in a meeting where consensus cannot be reached but is needed for a strategic decision to be put into action? What happens? Does someone suggest 'Why don't we send out a survey and ask the employees what they think?' Hence, the 'survey' has become the modern 'magic bullet' by which management quickly 'understands the needs' of any issue. This is true in product development, in marketing, in management information system (MIS), and may have originated in HR (employee development). Is survey feedback so simple that any manager can create a survey, identify the issues and solve the problem? How many times do we survey employees looking for answers or trends to organizational challenges? Now take that one step further. How often do we survey our own employees looking for answers as to how other employees (or organizational subsystems) can improve? Isn't this the premise behind 360-degree feedback in organizations? OD literature and modern business management practices suggest it is. The proliferation of survey feedback in organizations makes this an important topic to every manager. We may not be aware of the impact our survey-feedback processes have on productivity.

Organizational survey feedback

Among many other applications, 360-degree survey feedback is used as a change tool in performance measurement systems for employee development, career counselling and group development. It has functioned as a successful tool in organizations because it gives people information about the system in which they participate. Feedback is a central concept in productive system development. Consultants and 'change theorists' see the generation and use of valid feedback data about organizational functioning as the central defining characteristic of organization development (Argyris, 1970). As a result of feedback's centrality to productivity and successfully change, managers desire to know how to maximize its capability. One such way is to understand the 'feedback effect' in terms of a corporate capital. This was important at Fluid Corporation, the organization where I worked, because 'capital' is a term an executive committee member can relate to. What is unknown to most managers –and even survey feedback practitioners – is the *latent* effect that team feedback has on productivity. This latent effect can be characterized as 'stored capital' that produces or inhibits resource flow in a team, department, division, and/or an organization. It is easier to discuss the 'capital resource' implications of survey feedback in contrast to the 'behavioural intentions' produced by survey feedback.

Organizations are repositories of capital. This capital can be financial, intellectual, human and social. Capital resources flow through the organization as a result of social exchange between teams. This chapter is dedicated to helping managers recognize these resources, identify them, and understand how their decision to implement 360-degree survey feedback affects capital resource flow. A case example is provided to illustrate the moderating effect of feedback on capital. The following case is an actual company that implemented a 360-degree survey feedback process in hopes of improving productivity, inter-team relations and identifying best practices. As an executive in the organization, my role was to assess the effectiveness of the survey feedback programme across the entire organization and improve its applicability to the people, process and system. This example is now provided with key managerial insights noted.

Fluid Corporation and 360-degree survey feedback

Fluid Corporation (FC) is a global manufacturer of fluid components for commercial industries. Components such as premium faucets, valves, and precision pipe fittings constitute a bulk of FC's product line. FC employs more than 1,000 employees at its world headquarters just outside Milwaukee, Wisconsin, USA. The corporation has spent the past twenty years aggressively expanding international sales and manufacturing capabilities. It has manufacturing plants globally. The corporation is publicly held, but the originating family owns controlling stock. The company continues to expand operations globally, but still retains a familial culture. FC enjoys a dominant (60 per cent) leadership position in the fluid components market and has a strong track record of revenue, profit sharing and shareholder dividend growth. The success of the organization combined with the family-style culture engenders a conservative and practical work environment where employees are rewarded for the logical execution of strategic plans and operational activities. FC's market leadership position and financial resources are its strength as it expands into new global markets. The weakness of the organization is the complacency and risk-aversive inefficiencies that afflict many organizations achieving growth over several decades.

Industrial operations

FC's chief executive officer is the driving force behind the corporation's success. A visionary leader in the organization for more than twenty years, he has managed to keep initiative alive through a 'business unit' (BU) structure that promotes teamwork. The term *business unit* and *team* are used interchangeably in this chapter. Figure 5.1 illustrates this structure while identifying the primary function, size and earnings of each unit.

The primary corporate strategy is set by the CEO and carried out through a Management by Objectives programme (MBO). Corporate objectives are ultimately the annual performance metrics FC uses to compensate leadership and team members. As Figure 5.1 indicates, different metric systems are used with different business units. Manufacturing units focus on *delivery* as their main performance metric. Market development teams (MDTs) focus on *profits*, while sales units focus on *sales growth* as the primary performance metric. Manufacturing, marketing and sales units perform distinct activities within the organization. To be profitable, responsive and innovative, these

Fluid Corporation
Industrial US operations

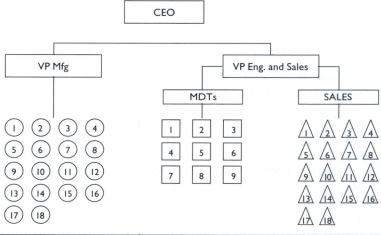

Work groups	Mfg Cell	MDT Team	Sales Office
Number of units	18	9	18
Grouped by	Product line	Market	Geography
Primary metric	Delivery performance	Profit	Sales growth
Average number of team members	20	12	6
Average $ of responsibility	6 million	15 million	6 million

Figure 5.1 Fluid Corporation organizational structure.

forty-five business units must efficiently interact and co-operate on corporate goals. Effective interaction results in a productive workplace. To identify, benchmark and improve interaction, management implemented a 360-degree survey feedback system. What I learned from participating in and assessing FC's process is that a survey feedback process needs to recognize more than organizational structure, it must recognize organizational drivers. In this case, delivery, profits and sales growth are primary drivers. Each team would use these drivers as their framework for to evaluate feedback. Their inter-team feedback was targeted at improving that driver. FC management was looking for a universal 360-degree survey feedback tool. What happened is each team took the universal tool and provided/interpreted feedback in reference to their driver.

The elusive benefits of teamwork

At FC, business units have their own profit and loss statements. They are independent operational entities, but rely on other teams to be effective, reach goals and survive. For example, a manufacturing BU could not achieve their delivery goals without the marketing and sales teams, and vice versa. From a structural standpoint the business units operate as a matrix organization. Teams are free to self-organize. For example, manufacturing, marketing and sales teams can collaborate around a given customer, application or product line. A single team cannot fully achieve its goals without the support of the other teams. This strong inter-team dependence makes the study of relationship moderation based on 360-degree survey feedback even more important. It became evident early, that the stronger inter-team dependency is, the more significant impact survey feedback has on resource flow between teams.

For feedback to be productive, it has to be specific, constructive and timely. To accomplish this at FC, management implemented a systematic feedback process administered through its global HR department. The 360-degree inter-team survey feedback process was officially known as the Quarterly Survey Feedback Process (QSFP). The QSFP produced formal communication quarterly between business units. Team members were able to qualitatively and quantitatively score other teams and relay opinions about how these business units performed. The QSFP served a dual purpose: feedback to teams from their peers, and a quarterly score by which to benchmark their performance. A business unit's ability to increase this score was linked to a performance pay programme. This rating system – a formal 360-degree survey feedback process linked to a performance pay system – provided a rich setting for action research. Linking a survey-feedback system to a performance pay programme in any organization accentuates the positive and negative effects of the system. At FC, this made understanding the QSFP even more important.

The QSFP had been established in 1997 and produced three years of complete data that I used for assessment in 2001. My action research was aimed at answering a single question for FC's management: does 360-degree survey feedback moderate resource exchange between team members? If this is true, subsequent questions are concerned with what resources are moderated? How may this affect organizational productivity?

My assessment of FC's 360-degree survey feedback process was conducted in participatory fashion using an acceptable and rigorous action research model. A brief review of action research is feedback systems sets the stage for my investigation and learning at FC.

Action research in feedback systems

Numerous survey feedback experts have noted that organizations often devote the least time to the feedback aspect of the survey feedback process, yet feedback can have the most impact (Nadler, 1977; Church and Waclawski, 1998). Understanding the impact of feedback requires understanding the context in which the feedback is presented and used. Understanding the results of feedback as they relate to context, constraints, intuition and most importantly actions is what Mackenzie (2000a, 2000b) identified as feedback with 'knobs'. Knobs are directional components resulting from the informational components of feedback. In this case 'knobs' are similar to the 'drivers' I suggested before. However, 'knobs' are actionable items of 'drivers'. For example, survey questions about profitability actions are 'knobs', but profitability is the *driver*. Knobs are the directional component that results in action or 'collaboration' between teams or business units. Methodology that discovers the key variables (knobs) affecting collaboration between teams at FC was first selected. An interview with QSFP participants was a natural first step. I wanted to really understand the process from the participants' perspective first. So I set up an interview protocol based on existing survey feedback assessment tools. A manager can easily access this on-line or through survey feedback professionals.

Use an interview protocol

Using prescriptive interviewing technique, I set up a series of comfortable discussions with fifteen key team members across fifteen business units: five manufacturing personnel, five product development (MDT) and five sales. These individuals were consistently involved with FC's survey feedback process. The quality of the interviews and subsequent data depended on knowledgeable interviewees who were willing to communicate. The interview protocol helped guide the discussion and compare answers. The questions were meant to understand interviewees' willingness to collaborate as a result of the QSFP. The interview protocol encompassed these major topical categories:

- participation and energy spent in the survey process
- interpretation and communication of feedback
- actions taken as result of the process.

The basis for these topical categories is Nadler's (1977) feedback system addressing participation, perceptions and behaviours resulting from survey feedback. Frequently, follow-up questions to an interviewee's story focused on resultant actions such as:

- 'What behaviour was demonstrated?'
- 'Why that behaviour?'
- 'What was the decision process?'

From these questions, interviewees could frequently recall the attitude or overall 'feelings' at the time of the feedback. Interviewees frequently would cite actions taken as a result of feedback. Verification of these actions helped triangulate and validate the data.

To triangulate the data, I conducted follow-up interviews with FC's HR department and executive group. The third leg of data triangulation was actual feedback data from the 1998–2000 QSFP. Interviews with HR and industrial executives focused on their experiences and interactions in the QSFP. As these stories emerged, greater detail was sought on the feedback process and results:

- submission of feedback properly and on time
- submission of constructive feedback
- submission of destructive feedback
- submission of feedback that was unusual or outside accepted norms
- processing of qualitative and verbal feedback comments
- resolution of misunderstandings as a result of the data
- complaints concerning feedback
- actions resulting from feedback
- intra-team communication of feedback.

The data set consisted of team feedback during 1998–2000. These data could also be used to cross-check interviewees' claims that a specific piece of data was given by a specific team. A minimum of two claims per team was researched. Of 128 claims checked, 117 (91 per cent) were found in the data set. This finding suggests that teams collectively have good recollection of previous survey feedback. This is important to any management team assessing a feedback programme. The programme needs to be studied from the participants' perspective, but cannot rely simply on compilation of participant verbatim. Participant comments must be grouped, themed, cross-checked and validated in a statistical and logical manner. From this variables can be identified, investigated and measured. Knowing which variables were important was actually step two. Step one was determining if the feedback process itself was perceived as important.

Do survey participants believe in the process?

Having studied the QSFP in detail, discussing it with the HR staff, I used the protocol to elicit the meaning that BUs were drawing from the process itself. Aside from content related to relationships, several other process variables emerged from the interviews. All interviewees agreed:

- the QSFP is a high 'visibility' process at FC
- QSFP forces communication between teams
- positive and negative feelings emerge as a result of the QSFP.

The QSFP is an inherently important operations mechanism to teams at FC. As one MDT leader stated 'the man gets what the man wants', referring to the fact that FC's CEO wants survey feedback on all BUs. Another sales team member commented that they understand it affects people pay and 'that alone makes it important'. BUs are forced to score one another, even in their operational interaction wouldn't warrant it. As one manufacturing leader stated,

> I don't blame them [sales BU] for scoring us incorrectly, they really have no idea what we do everyday . . . we have very few shipments to their office. What are they supposed to say about us?

Another sales BU member stated:

> Maybe it's [scoring every BU every quarter] similar to Robert's Rules of Order. You have to say something about the previous meeting. Now you could've decided something big, something small, or nothing at all . . . but you still have to say something about the minutes of the previous meeting. Whatever you say, someone is going to have an opinion about that, because it may be important to them. I guess, my point is that some things are better left unsaid; but our process won't really let that happen now will it?

One of most interesting early findings was in regards to BU members' awareness that feedback affects their relationship with other BUs. As one sales BU leader succinctly stated,

> When teams see scores about their performance, they are going to take it personally, no matter what you say. Good, bad or indifferent, that score is telling them what your BU thinks of theirs. People are going to take it personally, and respond in kind. That is just human nature!

These comments made me realize that people are providing feedback fully knowing it will affect available resources. More importantly, I learned the survey feedback process is perceived as an important process to the organization, which makes it more important to the team members. It is also perceived as a forced communication medium that will affect their relationship with the BU receiving their score.

During FC's survey feedback process assessment, one of my most interesting findings was the use of the word 'ding'. A *ding* represents a significantly low performance score. It is often the result of a specific incident or situation. The following examples provide insight into how the *ding* is perceived by those assigning and receiving feedback:

> After being in the middle of the pack [in regards to delivery performance]

our cell [team] made a huge effort to improve performance [delivery]. We put an extra person on assembly and had them help get every order out ASAP for an entire quarter. Overall, our survey scores improved, however we missed one shipment for one rep [sales team] and they dinged us! That isn't right! We can make 99 shipments on time, then get dinged for the one we miss. As I said, people remember your mistakes, not what you do right.

For us to sit and ding these guys would be counter-productive to the whole [QSFP] process. We don't want to tick anyone off, but if they [manufacturing teams or MDTs] mess up an important order, they deserved to be dinged.

A ding is a negative score? [heavy sarcasm] We had no idea a three would lower their pay. We scored them a three and they called us up and said 'What the hell did you ding us for?' I had no idea what they were so pissed about. To some degree it appears people are just looking for a damn grade.

Slam, hammer or ding . . . it don't matter. I don't ding people because it pisses them off. By golly, they deserve it sometimes but it isn't worth my people's time to deal with the crap that comes next.

Perhaps some teams are giving us perfect scores because they don't want to ding us money wise.

Fairness results from an expectation of what a score should be. A score that doesn't meet that expectation is defined as a *ding*. As a result of the ding, BUs take notice of who dinged them and what to do about it. BUs also noticed when an exceptionally good comment was written, but not when an exceptionally high score was given. The consensus was that high scores were expected. A review of process based motivation literature, such as expectancy theory suggests (Lawler, 1970), action results when rewards do not meet perceptions of fairness. My experience with FC's process was that people expected feedback scores and comments that would not punish them monetarily. If a low score or comments dragged their overall score down, they were 'dinged'. Every interviewer could provide an example of someone who 'dinged' them on the QSFP process. It was interesting to me that few interviewers commented about the great scores they received. This may suggest that feedback processes have more downside than upside when it comes to feedback. Perhaps, this is consistent with research that cites three critical comments are often made for every positive comment in typical employee development and survey programmes.

The key learning from studying the quarterly survey feedback process was a new understanding of the 'degree' to which employees were motivated by the survey feedback process. This can be overlooked by upper management, which tends to overestimate the degree to which employees 'commit' to organizational performance improvement programmes. In this case, I too had overlooked this fact. I was studying key behavioural elements, without understanding process *importance*. A simple but critical mistake to any research, focusing so much on the answer, that you forget to ask 'Does anyone care?' Or in the case of FC, 'How much do teams really care about the QSFP'?

The moderating effects of survey feedback on the system

After establishing that team members are energized by feedback and are capable of identifying the source of the feedback, I needed to discern whether team members moderate behaviour towards the feedback source. If behaviour is moderated, was it a productive or counter-productive moderation? A key component of action research is the use of data within the system to generate new and refined data. It is this research loop that produces practical answers to questions such as these. FC employees were asked as to the exact behaviours they took as a result of 360-degree feedback from their peers. Box 5.1 lists specific actions that team members would or would not take on behalf of other business units. These behaviours were specifically linked to actions taken as a result of inter-team feedback from the QSFP.

Team	Productive behaviour	Unproductive behaviour
Manufacturing	Tear down a set-up Assemble a rush order Same-day shipping Make a special	Reprioritize orders Do not quote Do not stock No free samples
Sales	Sell a specific product Push back rush orders Arrange customer visits Quote specials	No rush orders No priority shipping Change team priorities Sharing field note data Challenging pricing
Market development	Putting through rushes Applying discounts Raising commissions Urgent engineering Discontinue a product	Change commission Increase pricing Request free samples Discontinue promotions

Box 5.1 Behaviours resulting from survey feedback between business units.

In most cases, respondents' actions were stated in the future tense, for example, 'if they think we're going to rush their orders through, they are seriously mistaken . . . we bust our butts for them and look what happens.' Even more importantly, the common perception among BU members is that an incorrect score or a low score will result in unfavourable future actions. Many examples of potential social liabilities were given, a few are as follows:

They might say screw that [team], I'm not doing this.

Sure there is a fear bad feedback will come back to haunt us. It could be as minor as putting our order on the bottom of the list. Our fear is that we won't get support for other stuff down the road.

What will happen next time around? It's human nature he'll remember that!

We have to work with these people, we don't need enemies.

The perception is we could get stung [by the scores we give]. We don't want to get stung.

Survey scores make people do things they normally wouldn't.

I give [John Doe] high marks because he is difficult to deal with, and any other score will make him that much more difficult later on down the road.

What if that team has a leadership problem and they don't know how to use good or bad scores constructively? I can't take that chance because it will hurt our ability to get things done . . . It's painful to say that I don't think our leadership knows how to use scores [feedback] constructively and I don't think this process is accomplishing what it set out to do.

These examples are just a few of the most emotional responses garnered by the interviews. Only two of fifteen interviewees felt that the process was objective and that teams were professional enough to address scores in an objective way. One of these interviewees stated 'everyone has their personal problems and personalities, but in the end they have to act in a professional manner and treat them [scores] that way'. Significant counter-arguments regarding 'human nature', 'personality conflict' and 'politics' were given to suggest that BUs handled scores subjectively. A sales BU leader gave a good summary statement when he said 'We are all human and as humans we take exception to things. In this case it is feedback from other teams'. In summary, BU members participating in the QSFP believe feedback leads to action or a predisposition to act (intention). These intentions are the Social Capital (SC) or Social Liabilities (SL) of the receiving BU. They represent a 'resource' teams can or cannot call upon when needed. In an effort to materialize what an example of SC or SL would be, interviewees were asked to give examples of exceptional things they have done or could do for other BUs.

Box 5.1 exemplifies those activities resulting from behaviour intentions created by the survey feedback process. For example, if a manufacturing team was happy receiving positive survey feedback, they might be willing to tear down a set-up and replace it with another product run at the request of a sales or marketing team. Conversely, if they are unhappy with survey feedback, they may decide to not quote or stock a product the sales and marketing teams need. These can be 'not-so-obvious' day-to-day activities resulting from productive and unproductive behaviours resulting from 360-degree survey feedback programmes.

Creating a table of productive and counter-productive 'actions' was instrumental to conveying the effects of the 360-degree survey feedback process on resource exchange. It was useful to show employees how these activities affected organizational performance. It was useful to emphasize with management how each team holds the ability to increase or inhibit resource flow. Perhaps the most practical example I used with upper management was the example of a team not shipping a rush order the same day, because they had been 'dinged' by a sales team in the previous survey quarter.

Assessing a 360-degree survey feedback system

How do managers assess their own survey feedback programmes? We can start by questioning whether the 360-degree survey feedback system is stimulating productive and unproductive behaviours. To do this, we simply talk with participants and ask them how they are using the feedback. The degree to which participants care, in conjunction with the degree to which they take action or *intend* to take action, ultimately provides the indicators to us as to whether the system is impacting resource flow significantly.

Figure 5.2 depicts the survey feedback trait and state model. This illustrates the concept presented in the previous paragraph. Managers can use this model to begin assessment of their internal feedback systems. First, managers must determine the current 'trait' associated with survey feedback in the organization. Do employees care about the process? Research on the survey feedback system is required. What do employees think of it? Interviews using a structured protocol work very well here. The primary question a manager should answer is about motivation: 'Does our current 360-degree survey feedback process motivate?' If the answer is 'yes', which it will be in most organizations with a good HR/OD department, the need to assess 'attitudes' and 'behaviours' resulting from survey feedback is more warranted. Conversely, if people are not motivated by the process, they are less likely to take action on its behalf. This is fundamental to most process theories of motivation in the workplace (Lawler, 1970). Next, managers should understand the attitudes shaped by 360-degree survey feedback. Again, interviews can help accomplish this task, but a stronger methodology is to use existing survey instruments available through public and private organizations specializing in survey feedback. Attitude surveys about feedback processes provide managers with an empirical tool that can be critical in manufacturing/production environments where technical detail is the preferred data.

If teams are motivated, and the 360-degree survey feedback system is working, there are likely to be attitudes formed around the specific inter-team feedback. These attitudes manifest into behavioural intentions which are *potential* resources and liabilities to other business units. Because these behaviours may be latent, they act as a stored resource or liability. Employees may act immediately, or act a later time, when a specific team requires that employees efforts to satisfy a goal. An emerging stream of organizational researcher calls these stored system resources a form of social capital and social liability.

As Figure 5.2 illustrates, a 360-degree survey feedback programme will have a 'trait'. In other words, are employees motivated by the process itself? Managers often have a gut feel as to whether this is true or not. Next, is the 'state' of the process. If employees are motivated by the survey feedback process how are they reacting to the feedback. As managers, we want to understand the 'state' of the process. Good attitudes towards constructive feedback results in positive 'state' where behavioural intentions will likely yield social capital (resource access) for other teams. Poor attitudes towards inter-team feedback can result in a negative 'state' where behavioural intentions yield a social liability (resource denial) to other teams. Look at the model in Figure 5.2 and consider the importance placed on the process and the actual use of feedback by your employees.

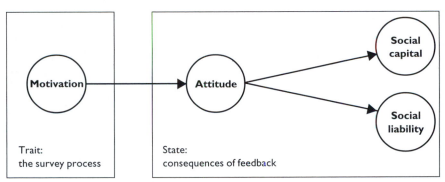

Figure 5.2 Survey feedback trait and state model.

What do the experts say?

This chapter is designed to help managers assess and build successful 360-degree survey feedback processes. It is based on the premise that the feedback employees provide one another has an impact on corporate performance. Central to this premise is the concept that feedback affects performance by moderating resource flow through the organization.

Upper management may question the factual nature of this premise. To support managers who need to rationalize the need to conduct an assessment of their internal feedback programmes, a theoretical summary of relevant organizational, management and business literature is provided in support:

- Organizations are systems that comprise subsystems, networked together by the need to belong and be recognized (Von Bertalanffy, 1968).
- Information shared between systems moderates the engagement of subsystems (Katz and Kahn, 1978; Kahn, 1990).
- Survey feedback is a widely used organizational process that creates information sharing between subsystems (Church and Waclawski, 2001).
- Survey feedback processes generate energy and produce both productive and counter productive behaviours (Nadler, 1977).
- Behaviours are conscious choices made by team members motivated by external stimuli in context of internal decision making (Lawler, 1970).
- Behavioural intentions are a result of attitudes towards a process or information source (Ajzen and Fishbein, 1980).
- Productive behaviours result from positive energy and attitudes generated by sub-system feedback (Nadler, 1977).
- Unproductive behaviours resulting from negative energy generated by sub-system feedback (Nadler, 1977).
- Efficient access to key resources through organizational relationships is a defining characteristic of successful individuals, teams and companies (Baker, 2000).

A manager's model: survey feedback and successful systems

This research presents an exploratory look into the moderating effects of 360-degree survey feedback systems on business units. It uses a case analysis of an industrial manufacturing organization as the experimental site. Case analysis results are difficult to generalize and are considered more speculative due to their limited scope. However, their strength is the actionable research, rich inquiry and practical model a single case analysis provides. Managers can learn, interpret and build about the model provided here. This research provides both a practical example for managers as well as a model for them to investigate survey feedback systems in their organization and begin to answer the question: 'Is our 360-degree survey feedback process increasing productive behaviours and organizational productivity?'

The survey feedback trait and state model provides managers with a model for survey feedback assessment in their organization. Upper management might react to this model by saying 'Why would we survey our survey process' followed by 'Do we really need feedback on our survey feedback process?' The answer is undoubtedly YES. If your organization relies heavily on 360-degree survey feedback for productivity improvement, personnel improvement and teamwork development, you should assess and calibrate the efficiency of that engine. If additional arguments are needed to justify the investigation, consider:

1   What is the time and cost of the survey feedback programme in your organization?
2   Has the programme grown or shrunk in the past five years?
3   What are the implications of excellent feedback and poor feedback? Does your organization know in terms of productive/counter-productive behaviour?
4   Has the survey feedback process achieved its goal? Does it have a goal?
5   Leaders can be trained to facilitate constructive feedback but can they identify behaviours and activities that result from survey feedback?
6   Is there evidence that participants know how to 'play' the feedback game? Do they score subjectively to ensure resource flow? (High scores across the board!)
7   How productive are we with the feedback that employees provide?

Your executive management team may argue that feedback on your feedback programme is redundant and perhaps ridiculous. Beware of this belief. The evolution of feedback communications systems in the modern-day organization is outpacing the training, implementation and reflective tools needed to utilize survey feedback properly. A system designed to identify, calibrate, share and optimize productive workplace behaviours –such as a 360-degree survey feedback system – has incredible power to increase productivity, or hinder it. We should all take the time to know which is true in our own organizations, even if we have to elicit feedback on our own survey feedback process.

References

Ajzen, I. and Fishbein, M. (1980) *Understanding Attitudes and Predicting Social Behavior*. Prentice Hall, Englewood Cliffs, NJ.

Argyris, C. (1970) *Intervention Theory and Method: A Behavioral Science View*. Addison-Wesley, Reading, MA.

Baker, W. (2000) *Achieving Success through Social Capital.* Jossey-Bass, San Francisco, CA.

Church, A. H. and Waclawski, J. (2001) *Designing and Using Organizational Surveys: A Seven-Step Process.* Jossey-Bass, San Francisco, CA.

French, W. L. and Bell, C. H., Jr (1999) *Organization Development: Behavioral Science Interventions for Organization Improvement.* Prentice Hall, Upper Saddle River, NJ.

Kahn, W.A. (1990) Psychological Conditions of Personal Engagement and Disengagement at Work, *Academy of Management Journal*, 33: 692–724.

Katz, D. L. and Kahn, R. L. (1978) *The Social Psychology of Organizations.* John Wiley, New York.

Lawler, E. (1970) Job Attitudes and Employee Motivation: Theory, Research and Practice, *Personnel Psychology*, 23: 223–227.

Mackenzie, K. D. (2000a) Knobby Analyses of Knobless Surveys Items, Part I: The Approach, *International Journal of Organizational Analysis*, 2: 131–154.

Mackenzie, K. D. (2000b) Knobby Analyses of Knobless Surveys Items, Part II: The Application, *International Journal of Organizational Analysis*, 3: 238–261.

Nadler, D. A. (1977) *Feedback and Organization Development: Using Data-Based Methods.* Addison-Wesley, Reading, MA.

Paul, K. B. and Bracken, D. W. (1995) Everything You always Wanted to Know about Employee Surveys, *Training and Development*, 49(1): 45–49.

Von Bertalanffy, L. (1968) *General Systems Theory: Foundations, Development, Applications*, revised edition. George Braziller, New York.

Chapter 6

Rejuvenating a mature service organization

Thomas Schmidt

The Company and its environment

The company, Neptune Shipping (Neptune), although sizeable in its niche market, is not a large shipping company by international standards, employing some 1,500 people and operating a fleet of six car ferries and sixteen container vessels. The term 'big fish in a small pond' could be appropriately applied to describe its position in the market. A recent publication described Neptune as a 'diversified shipping group specialising in the carriage of passengers, passenger cars and freight on a network of routes throughout the Baltic'. Although the freight business was more dependable, non-seasonal and growing, it had always been seen in many ways as the 'poor relation'. The company's history stretches back more than a century. In the relatively recent past however, its ownership changed from state control to the private sector. This change of ownership created the opportunity, and indeed the imperative, for the company to be restructured and modernized. Having gone though a period of more than five years of sustained losses, the state was no longer prepared to subsidize the company and when it was eventually sold to private investors, the need to restore profitability was made clear. Under private ownership the company no longer had the safety net of state subsidy and would either prosper or fail by its actions.

The market in which Neptune operated was dominated by a small number of players, all of whom protected their respective market shares jealously. Competition among these players was intense, driving market prices down to levels that were ultimately unsustainable in the longer term and often resulting in the weaker players being weeded out. The competitive environment could be described as a vicious circle of intense competition and inadequate returns, followed by a period of thinning out as weaker companies were forced out of the market. Then followed a period of some relief for the remaining industry players, but only until such time as spare capacity or low demand caused one or more players to break rank and commence the competitive cycle again.

The industry had few competitive secrets. All competitors engaged in the scrap for increased scale and improved market share. Differentiation as a competitive strategy was not considered a viable option, as most customers, particularly those involved in the freight sector and on whom Neptune relied for almost 30 per cent of its revenues, regarded the service as something of a commodity. By definition, the companies in the industry were long established. Many were jaded in their thinking and in their attitudes. In Neptune, our understanding of how we had managed to survive, how we had come through a prolonged period of loss making and the transition from state to private ownership, had a profound effect on attitudes and culture within the organization. These deep-rooted beliefs made change in the organization very difficult. Schein (1985) argues that organizational culture is deeply influenced by what members of the organization understand to have influenced the organization's survival. This results in a line of reasoning that runs – because we have survived, the way we do things must be right, therefore don't change the way we do things. In this way, the culture within our organization, a product of its survival and longevity, created inflexibility, a lack of willingness to change and strategic myopia.

Somewhat controversially, Baden-Fuller and Stopford (1993) suggest that there are no mature industries, only mature managers, a view that captivated my imagination and changed my thinking on how mature organizations can and should compete. The authors describe the 'stasis of maturity' and its effects on the strategy, structure and culture of an organization. At a time when Neptune was undergoing radical change immediately post-privatization, my understanding of the issues that can affect the success of such an undertaking was informed and influenced by the alternative approach to competition in mature industry that Baden-Fuller and Stopford (1993) advocate. Although they accept the importance that Porter (1980) attaches to cost leadership and scale in mature industry, they also describe how a number of companies in such circumstances were able to add elements of differentiation to their competitive strategies in ways that changed the rules of the industry. They describe how companies like Benetton, Richardson Steel and Toyota added supply chain excellence, innovation and quality to their respective product or service offerings in ways that changed their competitive landscapes. They concluded that rejuvenation is possible in mature industries if people are prepared to change and if the barriers that often affect change in a mature organization are removed. Their step-by-step approach to rejuvenation in a mature organization, involving galvanizing, simplifying, building and exerting leverage, assisted immeasurably in the success of the change project that I undertook in Neptune, a project that took place over the course of a two-year action-learning MSc programme.

Competitive strategy

The key question that Neptune faced following its privatization was how it would compete. It was clear that funds would be made available to develop the company if the board could be convinced that plans for development stood a reasonable chance of success. Having analysed the market, it was decided to invest in significant additional freight capacity, enabling Neptune to tap into the very significant economic growth that was forecast in the markets it served. Additional capacity would also give Neptune the opportunity to rebalance trade flows on the routes within its served markets. Some routes had been starved of adequate and suitable capacity for many years and in some cases business was forced onto other routes and services due to Neptune's inability to meet market demand. Low margins and a fear that a significant increase in capacity would destabilize the entire market had previously dissuaded Neptune and many of its competitors from increasing capacity to any significant extent.

In order to succeed, the investment in additional capacity would have to be well timed to coincide with the forecasted upturn in economic activity and the marketing of the additional capacity would have to be undertaken with a degree of flair and innovation that had not previously characterized marketing initiatives within the company. Although the investment in capacity could be justified on economic grounds, based on a well-established correlation between growth in demand for shipping capacity and growth in gross domestic product (GDP) in the countries which Neptune served, a degree of doubt existed in relation to Neptune's ability to attract and retain new customers. Many of these doubts centred on the ability and willingness of our staff to respond to the challenge of growing the business. It was clear that if we continued to treat our freight customers as we had done in the past, being indifferent to their need for adequate and suitable capacity and relegating them to off-peak sailings at times of high demand from the more lucrative, but seasonal, tourist car market, we would not succeed. This attitude towards our freight customers was embedded in the culture of the organization and would result in the failure of our plans to grow that segment of our business if not addressed.

The formal approach to analysing an organization and its environment that was part of the action-learning programme gave me the tools and vocabulary to identify the emerging issues and to communicate these issues to colleagues. There was a high degree of ambiguity in Neptune regarding the meaning of words and issues like strategy, culture and structure. A common understanding of these terms and what they meant for us as an organization had to be developed so that management could discuss these issues in a meaningful way. This was achieved through a number of management development programmes at which these issues were discussed and clarified. Ultimately, a consensus was built around the need for Neptune to follow a cost leadership strategy, on to which we would attempt to graft the pursuit of customer service excellence. We concluded that customer service excellence was something that the entire staff of Neptune would buy into and own. It also gave us some comfort to know that such a strategy would not add significant additional costs and so offend our fundamental belief in cost leadership. We wanted staff to adopt the pursuit of customer service excellence with enthusiasm and commitment to an extent that would set Neptune apart from its competitors and offer real and sustainable competitive advantage. The investment in hardware would, we hoped, be matched by a marked change in how we treated our customers.

Implementation strategy

Effecting change in any organization is difficult and particularly difficult when it is undertaken in a mature organization. As it transpired, the strategic decision to increase our capacity was relatively easy. Our decision to do so was supported by market analysis and the economic forecasts. Our decision to differentiate our services by excelling in customer service was also based on customer research that showed that our freight customers would appreciate and support our services if we offered capacity at times of peak freight demand and did so with a high degree of reliability. Changes in supply chain management techniques, the development of logistics management and the implementation of just-in-time manufacturing processes were analysed and supported our decision to address the reliability of our services and the manner in which we handled our customers. The reliability of the vessels that were added to the fleet was greatly improved through investment in their engines and manoeuvring machinery, making them ultra-reliable in the prevailing wind and sea conditions. Things became more difficult when the questions concerning how to implement our strategy, change attitudes and win the hearts and minds of people in Neptune had to be addressed. We were clear on what we wanted to achieve and why we wanted to achieve it, but less clear on how we would implement the change.

Buchanan and Boddy (1992) refer to the need to consider process as well as content when considering making changes in an organization. They make it clear that strategic change is not only a matter of deciding what to do (content), but also a question of deciding how to do it (process). The two issues are intrinsically linked and any strategic change initiative which fails to consider these issues in tandem is incomplete. Their view caused me to consider the question of process in more detail and to catalogue the range of options available in terms of strategy implementation. The options available to management range from the forceful implementation of strategies, when circumstances require immediate action and conditions and the balance of power allow the change agent to act in this way, to far more participative and inclusive techniques that often involve superior leadership skills, when seeking to change attitudes or corporate culture.

Under the very complicated circumstances that existed in Neptune immediately after the privatization of the company, internal politics were rife, as managers jockeyed for position in the new order and it was unclear as to who would lend their support to a change initiative. The situation was made more complicated by a heavily unionized workforce who, when the company was under state control, had frequently exercised their right to withdraw labour. It was unclear how staff would react to developing the business, particularly if it meant more work for them or a change in their conditions.

The intervention

During the first year of the action learning programme, which was essentially the diagnostic phase, I was able to analyse the organization and industry in which I worked. Using a variety of different models, I developed a series of specific action items, numbering sixteen in all, that sought to give some order and clarity to the task of changing and improving the organization. These action items dealt with implementing changes in strategy, structure and culture and did so in an incremental way, through a series of small changes, demonstrating that the 'big bang theory' of organizational change is not always appropriate in effecting, organizational change. It was my experience that change was achieved incrementally, through working diligently on a series of issues. Dealing with the intervention in this way enabled me to 'eat the elephant' one bite at a time. The actions are listed in chronological order as they emerged and developed over the diagnostic phase and as the writer subsequently tried to implement change.

Action 1: Seek to have cost leadership accepted by the senior management team as a competitive strategy

This initiative is self-explanatory and although it appealed to the majority of the senior management team, all did not readily accept it. Issues arose in relation to the impact of such a strategy on job security and pay and conditions as cost leadership was misunderstood and was regarded as being synonymous with low standards and low pay. Ultimately, however, the logic of pursuing cost leadership won out. Although the cost base within Neptune has been greatly improved in the intervening period, through the introduction of additional capacity and the attendant economies of scale, it would be untrue to say, even to the present day, that we have achieved a position of cost leadership. It would be true to say that we are moving in that direction.

Action 2: Define an appropriate service model to create superior customer service

Baden-Fuller and Stopford (1993) argue that mature companies do not have to rely exclusively on cost leadership in order to compete and cite instances where mature organizations added forms of differentiation to their product or service offerings in ways that did not offend their cost leadership ambitions. I followed this approach and, relying on customer research that suggested that customers would value superior service, characterized by improved reliability and better customer relationships, tried to develop a model that would be capable of defining and implementing appropriate changes in our service offering. Although we understood that delivering a quality service to our customers would offer some competitive advantage, it was less clear what quality service actually meant in our industry. Schmenner (1986), who defines the challenges that confront service providers in different industries, helped to resolve this issue. Schmenner's service matrix located Neptune in the service factory quadrant and highlighted, *inter alia*, the importance of getting capital investment decisions right, of properly scheduling service delivery, of paying attention to the physical surroundings and through good customer relationship, 'making the service warm'. In conjunction with Schmenner's model I used Shostack's (1984) 'service process blueprint' to analyse in detail each element of the service provided in order to identify where improvements could be made. This rather procedural approach to service improvement is very similar to how ISO standards and procedures are defined in companies and used to standardize the service provided. Non-conformance with the defined standards is investigated and the causes of non-conformance are then systematically eliminated. To complete the picture in terms of service design, a third and final model was used, which identifies the order management cycle (Shapiro *et al.*, 1992). By examining the order management cycle, service processes can be tracked across an organization so that all divisions within the organization that interact with the customer or that can impact on service delivery can be identified and specific service quality responsibilities can be assigned.

These models in turn allowed me to define appropriate service levels, establish service procedures and ways of dealing with non-conformance and finally, to assign specific responsibilities for the maintenance of standards in service related areas. The service model developed in this way was robust and delivered real service improvements.

Action 3: Change the culture of Neptune to support the cost leadership and service strategies being followed

I tried to bring about a change in the culture of Neptune. In order to excel in the area of customer service it was clear that staff throughout the organization would have to feel part of the initiative and would have to identify closely with the organizations objectives. The difficulty involved in changing the culture of a mature organization should not be underestimated. Schein (1985) argues that culture can be detected at three levels – cultural artefacts, shared values and basic assumptions. By uncovering the basic assumptions which members of an organization share, we begin to uncover the real corporate culture of the organization. Within mature industries basic assumptions which have developed over time will be more difficult to unravel, more difficult to understand and therefore more difficult to change. This is particularly true for successful organizations, where members of the organizations may attribute the success of the organization, in part at least, to the way they behave towards one another or the way they perceive their environment. Changing such a position is difficult, as the change agent has little to offer other than the uncertainty inherent in change of any type, in place of the comfortable certainty or stability of the status quo. Schein suggests that in the face of such uncertainty, organizations will rely on the behaviours and assumptions which worked in the past. Successful organizations in mature industries are, by definition, more likely to have built up a repertoire of such behaviours. Success reinforces and galvanizes the culture. The longer solutions seem to work, the more deeply they tend to become rooted in the culture. Many of our attempts to change the culture were at a superficial level and were unsuccessful. They dealt with cultural artefacts rather than the more fundamental issues. In initiating customer service programmes, making changes to staff uniforms and our corporate logo, for example, we did little to influence our culture, as the impact of such changes on the basic assumptions of our employees was very modest and had no lasting effect. It is clear to me that as Schein (1985) suggests, questions of survival and inclusion have a profound effect on our basic assumptions and have to be understood if corporate culture is to be influenced in any significant way. The corporate culture of Neptune did not change over the duration of the action learning, but my understanding of the factors that can bring about such change was appreciably improved.

Action 4: Secure access to time-chartered vessels as a means of reducing cost

Time-chartered vessels would give Neptune the lowest possible cost base. The crews of such vessels are typically non-European, many coming for very low wage economies. Neptune's vessels were and are to the present day manned by seafarers from within the European Union. Although the cost benefits of non-European crews were very significant, this objective was inconsistent with our desire to excel in the area of customer service. To pursue such an objective would have threatened our seagoing staff and alienated them to such an extent that morale and motivation would be fatally wounded and service improvements made impossible. It was only as a result of tabling the issue that the strength of staff feeling on this issue was understood by management. Further consideration caused me to compromise on this issue in order to maintain popular support for the overall change initiative.

Action 5: Work towards flatter organizational structure in Neptune to reduce cost and improve customer

Flatter organizations allow bureaucratic layers to be removed, usually middle management, thus generating cost reductions and often improved service as frontline staff, particularly those dealing with customers, are empowered to think for themselves and, within agreed parameters, make their own decisions. The logic of bringing the decision maker closer to the customer is irrefutable but this approach is not without danger. I advocated replacing our hierarchical structure with a flatter organizational form. There are many pitfalls to be avoided in this approach. First, hierarchies work and under certain circumstances are highly appropriate. The hierarchical form has in-built co-ordination and has clear lines of communication. Moving to a flatter organizational form requires the issues of co-ordination and communication to be addressed if the organization is to remain under control. Removing a layer of management can have disastrous consequences if one does not compensate by establishing a different means of co-ordination, usually based on the self-motivation and professionalism of well-trained staff. In addition one must ensure that cross-functional communication is developed to replace the communication that would have flowed up and down the hierarchical levels. Although flatter organizations have much to recommend them, given societal changes and the increased desire of people to control their own work environment, it is incorrect to assume that increased responsibility and empowerment is something that can be bestowed by management rather than something that is voluntarily accepted by people in the organization.

Failing to address these issues can create an organization with poorly trained staff, poor communications and inadequate co-ordination. Instead of making the desired move from Structure 1 to Structure 2, the organization could move to Structure 3, as depicted in Figure 6.1, often with calamitous results.

Action 6: Develop a more participative style of leadership to weaken resistance to change and as an important step in changing the culture of Neptune

Schein (1985) postulates that culture and leadership are the opposite sides of the same coin. It is reasonable to hypothesize therefore that in order to change the culture of an organization, the style of leadership must also change. In summary, I advocated a change to a more participative and collaborative style of leadership as an important step in overcoming the resistance to change that traditionally hampered strategy implementation. The development of such a leadership style could have positive cultural

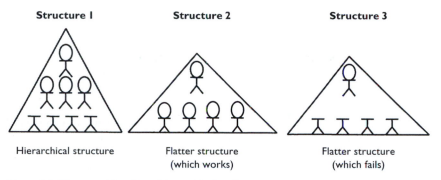

Structure 1   **Structure 2**   **Structure 3**

Hierarchical structure   Flatter structure   Flatter structure
                              (which works)   (which fails)

Figure 6.1 The transition from hierarchical to flatter structures.

effects and assist in bridging the gap of mistrust and suspicion that existed between management and staff. In order to achieve this objective a management development programme was put in place to assist managers in understanding their particular management or leadership styles and the effect that their styles can have on the culture of an organization. While the training programme itself was successful, it did not result in all managers making the transition and in a way defined the essential differences between managers and leaders.

Action 7: Seek to have the role of a transformational leader accepted and enacted by the CEO of Neptune

It was my belief that a transformational leader was needed to create and communicate a vision for the future Neptune, which would excite and energize people within the organization and which would paint a picture of the future that enabled them to *buy into* the vision and commit themselves to it. Kotter (1995) refers to the need to create such a vision and to the inadequate attempts made by the majority of organizations in communicating such a vision to their members. The prerequisites for achieving commitment from members of any organization to its vision are that the message being delivered is believed and that the vision is congruent with the hopes and aspirations of the employees on an individual basis. Therein lay the challenge for the transformational leader and indeed the challenge for Neptune, namely, to create a vision, which would act as a focus for all of the employees of the organization and help to co-ordinate the efforts of its various divisions. In an effort to make progress on this issue, I sought to influence the views of executive directors and succeeded in getting the CEO to talk more frequently and openly about his vision for the company in a way that resonated with staff at a more emotional level.

Action 8: Improve morale and motivation through goal setting and the development of suitable incentive-based reward systems

On observation during the course of the change initiative, it became clear that an assumption was made by management that staff shared their enthusiasm and ambition to improve Neptune. This assumption turned out to be incorrect. Staff who had not been involved in any meaningful way in the formulation of our plans initially regarded increased capacity as more work. Management had failed to engage them in the process and took it for granted that staff would simply row in, without having taken the time to communicate with them about our corporate objectives. I tried to deal with this lack of engagement in two practical ways.

Latham and Locke (1979) have researched the effect of goal setting on performance and behaviour and concluded that people perform better when they clearly understand their objectives and when specific targets are set . In setting specific targets for members of the CEO's team, I was able to engage staff in discussions about our overall objectives as an organization and at the same time agree realistic and measurable targets with team members that improved their individual performance and contributed to the achievement of our corporate objectives. As a secondary measure, I ironed out any anomalies that existed in the reward system for the staff and altered the bonus system so that the achievement of bonus was clearly linked to the achievement of defined and agreed objectives or goals. Both of these measures were logical, proved easy to implement and were very effective, yet in my opinion are often ignored by management.

Action 9: Seek to establish an independent or autonomous freight division within Neptune which will be capable of implementing the specific strategies needed to compete in the freight business

Neptune's freight business was historically perceived as an activity that was secondary to the more lucrative, but seasonal tourism business. As the company developed additional capacity, specifically to deal with surplus demand in the freight market, the relative importance of freight changed. The freight and tourism markets are very different. They have different customer bases, with different service demands and while the tourism market is very seasonal, freight demand is far more constant all year round. The extent of these differences convinced me that the interests of our freight customers would be better served if our freight and tourism interests were uncoupled and a newly formed freight division was given the freedom to pursue its own strategic objectives. Although the profile of the freight business was greatly enhanced during the course of the intervention and its autonomy increased, the argument for independence was not entirely won. The cost advantages involved in combining our freight and tourism businesses held sway and with the benefit of hindsight, it was the correct decision. In shipping, the utilization of available capacity is a key performance indicator. Combining freight and tourism traffics on multi-purpose car ferries enables Neptune to achieve high utilization factors, albeit at the expense of not fully meeting the competing individual demands of the freight and tourism markets in full. In the years that followed and as result of successfully developing our position in the freight market, the relative importance of the freight business in Neptune has increased and the balance of power between the competing interests of freight and tourism traffics has shifted.

Action 10: Seek to increase the involvement of middle management in the strategy formulation process in order to increase acceptance and assist implementation

I believed strongly that it was necessary to increase the involvement of middle management in the change process. Although senior management had agreed that as a company, we should concentrate on the delivery of low cost services, increasing our volumes by out-performing our competitors on service quality and reliability, it was clear that the delivery of that service and that the implementation of our plans would rest with middle management. We therefore sought to increase the involvement of middle management in the strategy process. Theoretically, this course of action makes good sense. It did not however prepare the company for the level of political manoeuvring that followed. Although politics are part of organizational life, politics can become dysfunctional and counter-productive. The level of such activity undermined my efforts to achieve a fuller involvement by middle management, as their energies were concentrated on how they would survive in a changing organization and how their place in the pecking order would also change. It became necessary to address the problem of dysfunctional politics before progress could be made.

Action 11: Improve the internal political climate by removing uncertainty and reducing competitiveness between members of the organization

Beeman and Sharkey (1987) suggest that the level of internal politics in any organization is a function of the competitiveness between members of the organization and the system uncertainties and complexities that exist. Understanding these factors assisted me in removing dysfunctional political activity to a very large extent.

In the uncertainty which prevailed following the privatization of Neptune, internal politics raged. Uncertainty continued to exist in relation to corporate strategy, bonus and reward systems, how to be successful in Neptune and many other issues besides. In addition to this uncertainty and perhaps because of it, Neptune became a very competitive environment in which to work, with little evidence of co-operation among middle management or between departments. Life in any large organization is complex and in Neptune it was no different, with added complexity arising from the rapid pace of change now being undertaken.

By removing uncertainties regarding the future of middle management in the organization, in effect by confirming to individual managers that they had a future and by clearly outlining the role that each had and the contribution that each would make, competition between middle management was quelled. Uncertainty regarding key issues like bonus payments, reward systems and promotion were clarified and slowly but surely the atmosphere in the organization began to change from one that was characterized by dysfunctional political activity and suspicion to one where co-operation and working towards team objectives became prevalent.

Action 12: Use backstaging techniques and an appropriate influencing style to build and maintain support for strategies within Neptune

Buchanan and Boddy (1992) suggest that the change agent has to support the 'public performance' of rationally considered, logically phrased and visibly participative change with 'backstage activity' in the recruitment and maintenance of support and in seeking and blocking resistance. They suggest that backstaging is concerned with the exercise of power skills, with intervening in political and cultural systems, with influencing, negotiating and selling and with managing meaning. Their description captures some of the difficulties and complexities involved in bringing change to any organization, and has much in common with Quinn's (1978) logical incrementalism and in particular the need to build and maintain the necessary support for any change initiative. Although accepting the place that backstaging plays in any change project, I learned that although influencing style and indeed the character of the change agent can influence the outcome of change projects, they are particularly difficult to modify. One who relies on rational/linear argument to influence does not easily change to ingratiation to achieve superior levels of influence. Similarly, if the change agent is open and communicative by nature, it is often difficult to change such habits to embrace more political influencing styles. On balance, I found Shakespeare's advice 'to thine own self be true' easier to follow and indeed more productive in the longer term in building trust and relationships.

Action 13: Seek to establish a better awareness of culture and the 'softer issues' among the management of Neptune

The so-called 'softer issues' often got bad press in Neptune. Management machismo and the preponderance of financially based performance measures sometimes got in the way of developing a clear understanding of how the softer issues like culture, leadership and motivation influence the performance of an organization. Ultimately, after initial efforts to introduce change failed because of the absence of staff support, it was accepted by the majority of managers that we could not simply 'manage' staff into compliance. Good management is not the same as good leadership and to improve as leaders our understanding of the softer issues that affect strategy implementation had to change and did change.

Action 14: Seek to have the importance of some non-financial performance measures recognized

Accountants and people with a background in finance dominated the board of Neptune. The difficulty in getting softer issues on to the agenda in such circumstances was considerable. The commitment of the individuals was not the issue, nor was their ability to understand the softer issues in a company. The problem arises from the manner in which each of us is influenced by experience in how we approach problems. We are enslaved by cognitive and cultural paradigms, which influence our judgement and determine the manner in which we approach and try to resolve problems. There was a difficulty in Neptune in seeking to have problems addressed in anything other than financial terms. There is evidence of this in the manner in which the restructuring and re-engineering of the company had been addressed. Great store had been put in getting the figures right and keeping the banks and shareholders happy. Resolving the behavioural issues that hampered the company's progress was put on the back burner. The question of whether or not it is possible to be successful as an organization by concentrating on financial issues alone is an interesting one. There is growing support for non-financial performance measurements which take the softer issues into account. Eccles (1991) suggests that there is mounting concern among management because of the inadequacy of conventional financial management systems in measuring the performance of an organization particularly in circumstances where the strategy of the organization should lead it to concentrate on areas of performance which cannot be measured in financial terms. Productivity, innovation, employee attitudes and public responsibility are cited as examples of areas of performance where financial measurement is either inadequate or wholly irrelevant. In recognizing the importance of some of the softer issues, the management of Neptune put systems in place to measure climate and staff attitudes and undertook training programmes that assisted in developing an understanding of the influence that leadership has on corporate culture. Our measurement of performance in dealing with the softer issues continues to the present day through staff surveys, 360-degree feedback and by undertaking regular management training programmes that enable managers to benchmark and update their leadership skills against best practice.

Action 15: Rely on logical incrementalism as an implementation strategy

Trying to manage the action items outlined above could not be done in a linear fashion. The interdependencies and complexities of some of the issues that have been discussed created uncertainty that made any linear approach to the problems that arose useless. Quinn's (1978) logical incrementalism accurately represents how I had to manage in the circumstances. Having tried to define an appropriate strategy and having sought to identify the resources and supports that would be required to achieve it, out of necessity I had to constantly re-evaluate the process and had to change course and compromise in the short term, in order to maintain momentum towards our overarching objective, precisely as suggested and advocated by Quinn.

Learning points, generalizations and conclusions

The entire MSc action-learning programme was an enriching and rewarding experience, both personally and organizationally, and taught me many valuable lessons. Some of the more significant learning points are outlined below.

- There are no mature industries, only mature managers. The ability exists for all mature organizations to redefine how they choose to compete. By closely tracking changes in its external environment, forms of differentiation can be identified that complement and support cost leadership.
- Dysfunctional political activity in an organization often derives from uncertainty and excessive competition among members of the organization. Removing such uncertainty and excessive competitiveness by clarifying objectives and the future role that members of the organization will have, reduces the organization's propensity to dysfunctional politics and allows members of the organization to concentrate on more productive issues.
- Logical incrementalism really works. The approach that I took to strategy implementation in Neptune was along these lines and proved largely successful.
- Understanding corporate culture is of particular importance in mature organizations. Schein (1985) describes corporate culture as an organization's response to the dual problems of external adaptation and internal integration. External adaptation is the manner in which the organization solves the problems of surviving in its external environment. Internal integration is the manner in which the organization deploys its internal resources to meet the challenges of the external environment and the manner in which the people within the organization behave towards one another. In mature industries the external environment is stable and in

the main, organizations will have learned how to understand and deal with the problems of external adaptation. In such circumstances the issues that determine the survival of the organization are more likely to be internally generated, such as how colleagues behave toward one another, how the reward system works, how one gets and maintains power and the criteria that govern exclusion or inclusion in the organization or group. Because corporate culture is so deeply rooted in mature organizations these issues are often more difficult to unravel and understand.

- Rejuvenation is possible in mature organizations. Baden-Fuller and Stopford (1993) claim that rejuvenation is achieved by doing something different, by being innovative and by making creative plays. A number of steps have to be taken in order to become an entrepreneurial organization as advocated by these writers. The process requires both radical and incremental change – radical in the sense that beliefs are altered and structures are torn down, skills modified and new technologies introduced. It is also incremental in the sense that for any organization which has limited resources change must be undertaken from within in a way which does not take unnecessary risks. Rejuvenation cannot be achieved in one leap and the authors cite instances where rejuvenation has been an iterative process stretching over ten years. Baden-Fuller and Stopford's approach to rejuvenation provided me with the idea and the methodology to change the way in which Neptune competed in the freight market and proved practical and effective. It allowed us to be innovative in developing a service strategy while at the same time respecting the necessity to protect our cost position.

References

Baden-Fuller, C. and Stopford, J. (1993) *Rejuvenating the Mature Business*. Routledge, London.

Beeman, D. and Sharkey, T. (1987) The Use and Abuse of Corporate Politics, *Business Horizons*, March–April: 26–30

Buchanan, D. and Boddy, D. (1992) *The Expertise of the Change Agent*. Prentice Hall, London.

Eccles, R. (1991) The Performance Measurement Manifesto, *Harvard Business Review*, January–February: 131–137.

Kotter, J. (1995) Leading Change: Why Transformation Efforts Fail, *Harvard Business Review*, March–April: 59–67.

Latham, G. and Locke, E. (1979) Goal Setting – A Motivational Technique that Works, *Organizational Dynamics*, Autumn: 68–80.

Porter, M. (1980) *Competitive Strategy*. Macmillan, New York.

Quinn, J. B. (1978) Strategic Change: Logical Incrementalism, *Sloan Management Review*, 20(3): 7–21.

Schein, E. H. (1985) *Organizational Culture and Leadership*. Jossey-Bass, San Francisco, CA.

Schmenner, R. (1986) How can Service Businesses Survive and Prosper? *Sloan Management Review*, 27(3): 21–32.

Shapiro, B., Rangan, K. and Sviokla, J. (1992) Staple Yourself to an Order, *Harvard Business Review*, July–August: 113–122.

Shostack, L. (1984) Designing Services to Deliver, *Harvard Business Review*, January–February: 133–139.

Chapter 7

Living up to expectations

Unexpected possibilities, unexpected benefits

Mary Lou Kotecki

The health care industry in the United States is faced with persistent, frequent and often dramatic change. Changes in health care technologies and practices, in environmental conditions such as competition, reimbursement mechanisms and marketplace economics, and in governmental and regulatory requirements provide constant pressure on organizations not only to survive but also to succeed. In recent years the industry reshaped itself through mergers and acquisitions of major health care corporations, hospitals and other entities. During this time complexity increased in part due to shifting health care relationships and escalating health care costs. So too changing political support of health care initiatives, lack of recognition of health care accomplishments by media sources, accelerated business growth and rising customer expectations demanded flexible, but effective approaches to patient care and family services. Generally speaking, a company's commitment to customer service requires a robust, timely and yet standardized approach to meet rising customer expectations. This effort is no small task, and services must constantly undergo enhancements to retain customer loyalty.

The health care industry is comprised of many sectors including health care providers such as hospitals and physicians, pharmaceutical services, insurers, laboratories and others. Among these sectors are health care companies that serve as health maintenance organizations (HMOs). Many of these organizations offer managed health care products and services to hundreds of thousands of members through employers (individual companies) and through state and federal government agencies that sponsor programmes such as Medicare for elderly people and Medicaid for people needing assistance.

The challenge

One health maintenance organization established in the mid-1980s serves over half a million customers in Midwestern and Southeastern states. Interestingly, this relatively young company is a wholly owned health care subsidiary of a company primarily recognized as a manufacturer. As a subsidiary of a major corporation, it works to reflect the positive image nurtured for decades by its parent. Although this health care company's approach to leveraging change differs from its sister divisions in a number of ways, the essence of its success does not. Since 1999 this health care organization attained the highest rating possible for HMOs within the United States for quality care and customer service as determined by the National Committee for Quality Assurance.

In 1997 this organization faced a crisis. It had experienced double-digit membership growth for a number of years. To accomplish this growth the company expanded geographically, increased its product offerings and nearly doubled its staff. In an attempt to continue its growth pattern, it chose to fund costly, new health care related ventures including construction of a number of new health centres and development of leading-edge computing technologies for managing patient information across medical entities and for data analysis. Costs associated with these efforts combined with enormous industry change caused the company to face a sudden, unanticipated loss. Fortunately, the organization was able to return to financial stability almost immediately. It did so by divesting initiatives not aligned with the company's strategic intent, by making significant improvements in performance of high quality, cost-effective products and services, and by refocusing on its major strengths – customer and health care partner relationships.

From its beginnings this organization had gradually improved its ability to 'listen' and to 'learn' from customers and partners. Member satisfaction surveys, provider interviews and employer visits were conducted with some regularity and results were analysed and acted upon. Following this time of crisis these skills led the company to understand the need to return to the local, more personalized customer services that had been its hallmark early in its history. At the same time the company sought to explore cost efficiencies through out-sourced processes. Beginning in 1998 the need for three inter-related action research endeavours became apparent: decentralizing customer service, creating a vision of future customer services and deploying its key elements, and finding a business partner who offered cost-effective capabilities for assuming major operating process responsibilities.

The first challenge issued to me, as vice-president for customer services, was to plan and deploy a move from a centralized customer call centre to decentralized call centres within the span of eight weeks. The short time-frame to accomplish this significant change was chosen in order to have reconfigured services in place prior to the upcoming membership enrolment period. Such an effort entailed creating call centres in multiple locations across the United States that were staffed with fully trained employees and which had appropriate call centre technologies installed and fully functioning.

In essence, 60 per cent of the work done by centrally located customer service representatives had to move to the field. To accomplish this move, current employees had to be transferred to field offices where possible, and new employees needed to be hired and trained for field positions. This change required reporting relationships to be redirected to from corporate central offices to field managers dispersed in multiple states. And, it required that those managers reporting up through marketing, not a customer service hierarchy, have a common vision for enterprise-wide services, performance levels and measurement. So, too, it was essential that a collaborative work environment and knowledge transfer process be established between current knowledge workers and new workers. Lastly, adoption and implementation of standardized processes for interdepartmental coordination of information and work was necessary for business to move forward primarily between call centres, member enrollment, nursing, claims payment and provider contracting areas. All of these changes had to occur without disruption in customer service.

Taking action

Because this organization had another strength – years of experience with facilitated action research-type activities – I quickly formed a team comprised of customer support and customer service managers and supervisors from across the company to develop and execute an action plan. We began exploring potential call centre redesign immediately by gathering internal call centre data as well as research information from external companies. This research included investigating companies listed as best call centres for 1996 and 1997 as well as reviewing results of benchmarking studies conducted by the International Benchmarking Clearinghouse. Among companies studied were other health care organizations, telecommunication companies, insurers, marketing groups, computer companies, manufacturers, financial institutions, retailers, publishers, airlines, newspapers, utility companies, hotels and travel companies. These included organizations with familiar names such as IBM, AT&T, United Parcel Service, Dell Computers, Cigna and London Free Press.

Summary customer service statistics from within the health care organization provided detailed insight on call volumes by hour, day, month and site-relationship as well as data on callers, call types, productivity per person and after-hours coverage. In addition, aggregated data outlined general and key customer requirements and expectations. An assessment of current technologies and technology support indicated an immediate need to add or improve phone lines and phone and computer technologies at remote sites. Capabilities needed included networked call centres (computer and telephones systems including interactive voice response), Internet/intranet environments, fax, a scheduling system for planning, scanners for letters, routing capacity, contact management system, real-time information on enrolment and eligibility, links to data storage and retrieval, and system statistics.

Concurrently, I led the team's effort to assess the internal implications of the change. Through a stakeholder analysis we identified key stakeholders and the position each group or person would take on this change. We also met with the company president and other company officers to determine the level of commitment and support they afforded to the change initiative and to confirm the scope of this effort and the expectations associated with outcomes. It was apparent that other issues required immediate attention.

Internal politics for power and control became evident within mid-level management levels. Although we found field managers eager to assume new customer-related responsibilities, they were resistant to seeking common approaches and to attaining targeted company wide performance levels for services. Because these managers were key to the success of the project, we began immediately to fully engage them in the project through a series of conference calls. Call discussions provided a means for explaining assumptions and requirements, clarifying misperceptions, gaining knowledge from field insights, reasserting the need for attaining targeted service levels, testing levels of commitment, and finally, getting concurrence on deliverables, implementation time lines, activities and supporting behaviours. These calls were part of a carefully developed communication plan. Among my roles were responsibilities to ensure that calls included the participation of key influencers in calls, that discussions kept on track, and that decisions were based on facts and data and aligned with project deliverables.

The decision to make so dramatic a change in services had a major impact on people staffing the centralized service area. Fear of job loss and fear of diminished career opportunities were a natural outcome of the change announcement. Direct, open discussion with all call centre employees through an all-hands meeting provided me with a means of explaining the need for the change and its potential effect and to ask employees for their help and support. This session offered everyone with an open forum to ask questions of me regarding any aspect of the initiative. Call centre managers and supervisors continued to discuss the change and its implications at subsequent staff meetings.

Following these discussions, I conducted a change readiness assessment using radio frequency-type devices to assure anonymity of responses. The assessment sought to learn call centre employee attitudes, norms and perceptions regarding three areas related to the impending change: credibility, organizational impact and individual impact. Credibility questions touched on topics such as the organization's support of prior changes, commitment to change, resources, abilities and skills. Organizational benefit/risk questions sought to learn 'what the changes mean to us' in areas of communication and information sharing, community and culture, customers, resources, work progress and expectations. Individual benefit/

risk questions focused on 'what the change means to me' with regard to personal impact, work levels, security, rewards, training, support and opportunities. This assessment identified building blocks that offered opportunities for successful change and stumbling blocks that needed to be overcome. An overall acceptance quotient indicated that, although employees were personally worried about their future, they understood the need for change, trusted the organization to support them in the best possible way, and were committed to facilitating successful change. These results were shared with each individual, and employee discussions continued as project implementation steps progressed.

Learning from research and assessment efforts combined with detailed discussions with regional directors and company officers enabled an initial redesign to be proposed. The team determined that the intent to serve members, providers, employers and government agencies, and internal inquiries with a sense of local presence required development of regional mini-call centres, two local site-specific call centres and a home office centre. As redesigned, staffing for these areas included customer and provider (physician) service representatives, special investigators, a supervisory staff, and access to support staffs such as nursing and benefit interpretation. To constrain operating costs, the total number of employees within these service centres was not to exceed current staffing levels.

As redesigned, the home office location would continue to serve not only members in its region, but also it would cover regional call centres during site staff meetings or weather-related closings. In addition, it would continue to facilitate claims inquiries, handle responses during off-hours and those related to foreign languages, hearing impaired, national accounts and other specifically identified areas. The home office location also would continue to carry the responsibilities to train and educate employees and members, as needed, to formally report measurements, to support audits by external entities, and to seek standardization and simplification of service processes across the company.

To my surprise, one of the critical elements of call centres – phone system technologies – became an obstacle of considerable proportion. An assessment of phone technology capabilities indicated a need to quickly upgrade specific field location in order to handle call volumes and response times. Various phone companies provided service to field office locations, and these companies responded with varying degrees of assurance that upgrades would be completed on time. To handle this urgent situation, I deployed the manager of the centralized customer service centre and a phone system consultant. They laid out a detailed plan to meet project deadlines and worked on a daily basis with companies across three states to shepherd installation of needed lines and equipment.

The communication plans deployed effectively gained approval of proposed changes from corporate and regional leaders and from employees impacted by the change. Proposed changes were communicated with varying frequency to department and site management, to regional and corporate marketing groups, and to all employees through different communication mechanisms selected for their effectiveness with each stakeholder category.

In the end, the redesign was implemented as planned within the allotted time period. No individuals lost their jobs, although some transferred to new locations. New employees were trained and mentored. Processes and measurements were agreed to and carried out. Technologies were installed following a transition plan. This massive effort encompassed many departments, management consensus, demonstrated leadership, and external organizations such as phone and technology companies. All locations went 'live' at the same time. No diminishment in performance occurred. Call abandonment percentages dropped to benchmark levels, and call inquiry resolution rates approached targeted goals. In fact, productivity increased and subsequent surveys indicated an increase in both employee and customer satisfaction.

Creating possibilities

As it turned out, identifying and acting on customer service expectations offered just a beginning. Action research, as a generally described approach to organization development, necessitates involvement of a number of key stakeholders from throughout the company in identifying a problem or opportunity, understanding underlying factors, planning based on diagnosis, executing actions, and evaluating the process and outcomes. Often, the learning that occurs in action research leads to another initiative. In this case, as a number of people gathered to work through customer service redeployment decisions and the development of communication and implementation plans, new learnings surfaced and ideas emerged. Early discussions within the organization moved from 'what service do we need to deliver' to 'what service do we want to deliver' and service delivery plans began to identify 'quick technology hits', integrated operating system implications, and sequenced and prioritized technology solutions.

Four months after the successful launch of mini-call centres, I convened a planning group that included individuals from various functional groups to envision the future of customer services and customer relationships. To accelerate and expand the potential for uncovering potentialities, I led the group through an appreciative inquiry. Session outcomes were simply summarized under the following headings:

- How did we get here? (purpose of redesign, what it takes to 'win', loose ends);
- Where are we heading? (seamless service, what do we mean by 'seamless' and by 'quantity and quality');

- How do we get there? (process maps and process understanding, best practice approaches, current gaps);
- How will we know when we get there? (internal and external measures and benchmarks);
- What does the future look like? (proactive servicing, continuous service improvements, future technology tools);
- Future interventions?;
- Communication plans?

This visioning session triggered powerful positive images of possibilities. It provided clear illumination of specific customer requirements and expectations. It identified means of not only improving customer services, but also of enhancing member, provider and employer relationships in ways that would differentiate this HMO from competitors. The inquiry acknowledged the company's dependency on the knowledge and skills of its call centre staffs. This realization triggered discussions on staffing size to achieve service goals, staff empowerment, training and education, call monitoring for purposes of mentoring and improving performance, and staff rewards and recognition. These results convinced the company president that the service areas should be structured to provide employees with a career path. The limitations of current job structures, in part, had caused personnel turnover in customer service areas to reach 37 per cent annually. Often employees applied for other more highly graded positions in other functional areas. To remedy this situation, I worked with Human Resources to create and implement job families that began at entry-level service positions and which linked to through increasing levels of responsibility to a directorship. In this endeavour, one middle manager resisted a grade increase for supervisory positions and argued against implementation – again a control issue. After considering these arguments for some period of time, the senior leadership group approved and implemented the new structure as originally recommended.

During this time the organization also felt pressured to seek means of reducing costs and of finding a way to fund a new multi-million dollar integrated operating system. Examples of cost cutting abounded in the health care industry through mergers and partnerships. The parent company had followed a path taken by many other companies steadfastly to increase outsourcing of various functional processes over a number of years to achieve cost targets. As a result, one of the HMO's senior vice-presidents launched a major effort to find a potential business partner who could provide robust integrated integrating operating system capabilities and through which customer and provider services and selected administrative functions could be outsourced. At the same time, information technology companies who marketed major integrated operating systems were invited to demonstrate their systems and to provide insight on system advantages, disadvantages and costs. As the company officer whose employees would most likely to be impacted by the potential outcomes of any outsourcing, I served as member of a small team who solicited and assessed external capabilities and costs. As partnerships and technology company proposals were submitted, they were analysed and presented potential proposals to the president and his staff for decision. My self-imposed role was to ensure that all facts and data were accurately and completely presented without bias, that a full range of possibilities were explored, that previous action research learning was considered, and that internal capabilities were made visible, clearly understood and fully appreciated. This role was critical in that efforts to persuade senior leadership to accept outsourcing were being advocated by some as an avenue for self-promotion and gain.

After a year of gruelling analyses, discussions, debates, political manoeuvring and concern, it became apparent that no external company could offer services at costs below those experienced within the company. Most importantly, we discovered, as I had long advocated, that any external company would be forced to hire the company's current employees in order to gain the knowledge necessary to efficiently carry out complex customer services with such high performance levels. Based on these findings, the company chose to purchase and install an integrated operating system plus a new integrated customer service system that would enable speedy, accurate and complete customer response through ready access to information, elimination of manual claims entry and enhanced communication across multiple functional groups. Nearly 400 jobs remained within the organization following these decisions, and the organization expanded its capabilities significantly through technologies.

As work progressed on these three overlaid action research endeavours, the company moved aggressively to identify and confirm its strategic intent and core competencies. It came to the realization that 'customer delight' was one of the fundamental elements of its strategies and tactics. Meeting or exceeding customer expectations became a driving force to guide and support development and implementation of our core competencies, attainment of our strategic intent and goals, and an avenue for delivering value that is visible to customers. Happily, I was charged with leading customer advocacy. In fact, my staff created a game-based learning approach entitled 'The Road to Delight City' to teach all employees about customer relationships, expectations, contact behaviours and responsiveness.

The art of continuous invention and learning

Through the years this HMO organization has experienced continuous, accelerated change caused in part by environmental and industry changes, double-digit membership growth, product line complexity and expansion, and customer and parent company expectations. Brown and Eisenhardt

(1997) found that for some organizations persistent change appeared to be a critical factor in the firm's success. The company discussed in this chapter learned to adapt to or leverage change for competitive advantage by recognizing and exploiting various important elements of its character and capabilities. It also maintained a steadfast focus on its vision and demonstrated an unrelenting pursuit of new ideas, a willingness to learn from itself and others, continuous improvement and growth. This company had worked through all organizational levels to achieve bonding, creating working teams, co-ordinating and adapting as outlined by Rashford and Coghlan (1994). In a sense, without deliberately planning to do so, it had accomplished this change in a manner described by Rashford and Coghlan as the adaptive coping cycle: sensing environmental change, acting on information, changing processes based on learning, implementing improved services, and soliciting feedback on change success.

Meeting the challenges facing the organization and attaining outlined goals under very severe time constraints required repeated action research cycles of diagnosis, planning, implementation, data gathering and analysis, learning and decision making, and identification of new actions. Implied in such steps was the wise and repeated use of internal and external feedback methods (Nadler, 1977). These efforts necessitated interventions with and active engagement of all levels of the organization – individual, team, interdepartmental and organization – into integrated solutions. Interventions needed to consider and accommodate all elements outlined in the Burke-Litwin Model of Organization Performance and Change: external environment, leadership, culture, systems, practices, mission/strategy, structure, work climate, motivation, tasks, individual needs and values, and performance (Burke, 1994).

The appreciative inquiry approach taken in visioning sessions led the group involved to reaffirm positive experiences, strengths, individual and organization potential while acknowledging notable attributes of other companies (Cooperrider et al., 2000). The inquiry also enabled exploration of possibilities as well as providing sufficient structure to determine and design implementation of key elements of future customer services and customer relationships.

Although Van de Ven and Poole (1995) note that, while organizations struggle to manage unfolding events as a course of conducting business, attempts to explain such change processes encounter difficulty as well, the basis for this organization's success is apparent. All of this work had as its underpinnings an understanding of the concepts of 'process' to attain value and performance. In fact, the organization's culture is based on a strong foundation in quality management and organization development, as defined in the broadest sense, an integrated planning system, a team structure, and a dedication to a customer and process focus. Every individual knows which customers he or she serves and understands business processes and related individual and organization performance goals. This foundation provides both flexibility and agility in adapting to and, in some cases, leading change.

As advocated by Bartunek *et al.* (2000), these action research interventions were led from a management level. I led the first two interventions, and a senior vice-president led the third. I found that meeting the challenges facing this organization required applying techniques and interventions from a variety of organization development approaches interchangeably, as required, to continue moving forward beneficially for individuals and the organization. Although the politics associated with outsourcing occasionally took on the aura of a spectacle, I dealt with them in a straightforward manner by listening to and openly discussing arguments for opposing positions while always ensuring the inclusion of facts and data within discussions. Lastly, I arranged for leaders, managers, external companies and others to view current service activities and to attend demonstrations of implementation enhancements. I took these steps so that performance, competencies, capabilities and costs would be self-evident. In this way, each person – those in a decision-making position and those who performed the work – could see that the potential value of changes had been realized, and that the changes had, in fact, delivered more benefits than had been envisioned. In 2003 one independent third-party survey of health care organizations indicated that this organization ranked second in the nation in customer satisfaction for customer service and support.

References

Bartunek, J. M., Crosta, T. E., Dame, R. F. and LeLacheur, D. F. (2000) Managers and Project Leaders Conducting their own Action Research Interventions, in R. T. Golembiewki (ed.) *Handbook of Organizational Consultation*, 2nd edition. Marcel Dekker, New York.

Brown, S. and Eisenhardt, K. (1997) The Art of Continuous Change: Linking Complexity Theory and Time-Paced Evolution in Relentlessly Shifting Organizations, *Administrative Science Quarterly*, 42(1): 1–34.

Burke, W. W. (1994) *Organization Development: A Process of Learning and Changing.* Addison-Wesley, Reading, MA.

Cooperrider, D., Sorensen, Jr, P., Whitney, D. and Yaeger, T. (eds) (2000) *Appreciative Inquiry: Rethinking Human Organization toward a Positive Theory of Change.* Stipes, Champaign, IL.

Nadler, D. (1977) *Feedback and Organization Development: Using Data-Based Methods.* Addison-Wesley, Reading, MA.

Rashford, N. S. and Coghlan, D. (1994). *The Dynamics of Organizational Levels.* Addison-Wesley, Reading, MA.

Van de Ven, A. H. and Poole, M. H. (1995) Explaining Development and Change in Organizations. *Academy of Management Review*, 20(3): 510–540.

Chapter 8

Improving influence and performance in a multinational subsidiary

Paddy McDermott

Context

Optix Ireland is a multinational subsidiary, manufacturing optical devices in the west of Ireland headed up by me. The period under observation is the activity from 1997 to 1999, when I was involved in the Irish Management Institute/Trinity College Dublin MSc Programme in Management Practice – an action learning programme. I had managed the operation from its start-up in 1994. At the time it had 200 employees and manufactured 20 per cent of worldwide demand. The plant was one of three in the group, which were organized on a regional basis. The size of the plant reflected the relative sales in Europe. Florida was the location of the head office and North American manufacturing headquarters. It had 600 employees and manufactured 75 per cent of the product. Australia supplied the Asia-Pacific region.

Optix Ireland was the European manufacturing headquarters and all products for the European market were processed there. The output from Optix Ireland required further processing by optical companies which were located throughout Europe. The product came in both generic and speciality forms with the generic products following a normal supply pattern. On the other hand, speciality products followed more of a sub-contract pattern.

Despite the plant's early successes, performance had deteriorated in the face of increasing complexity, a point which will be explained in the next section. Cost performance in Ireland was similar to the other regions but there were two new plants being set up in 1997. One, in São Paulo, was to supply South America, while the other in the Philippines was being set up to consolidate manufacturing of generic products worldwide. This was a direct threat to Irish volumes and as the business was experiencing difficulties, it was a considerable concern to me that the new low-cost facility in Manila would take greater volumes from the Irish plant.

Emergent issue

Against this background it was important for the plant to arrest the decline in performance and seek ways to consolidate its future as the main supplier to the European region. The company had moved from a centralized structure, with the plant managers reporting to the vice-president of worldwide operations, to a regional structure. The plant now reported to the European managing director as opposed to the vice-president of operations. So the environment was changing rapidly.

The organization change was driven by a desire for faster growth and it was seen that the regional focus was taking the business closer to the customer. As director of operations for Europe, I now had responsibility for customer and technical service for the region. But the change decreased the autonomy of the Irish plant. I perceived this loss of autonomy as a diminution in status for both me and the plant.

With a background in start-up situations, my style was entrepreneurial in approach. Mintzberg (1983), in his analysis of organization types, describes the 'simple structure' as the seminal form. In this type of organization the entrepreneur is central to all communication and activity, making all of the decisions. It is the most basic form of organization and is extremely effective and results driven. Unfortunately, as complexity increases, the simplicity of the structure cannot cope with the demands placed upon it. It was a good time for an action learning experience!

The story

The year 1997 was a time of great personal turbulence for me. Having worked very hard to establish good performance initially, the emphasis for the plant was changing and it was also under-performing. I felt particularly isolated because my style was results oriented. My focus had always been geared towards sorting out issues internally, rarely considering outside resources or help. But with the environment changing so much, it became impossible not to consider what was happening in the rest of the organization.

Taking stock of my situation, I didn't have a strong team supporting me at the plant. This lack of support was somewhat style induced. Being the central figure in a 'simple structure' didn't give them much input to the process. This needed to change if we were to address some of the operational issues. We had always maintained a strong focus on cost but were not as effective in maintaining good service to the market. With the change in environment and the desire for growth in the organization, service quickly became the main focus. The product portfolio had and continued to expand rapidly. The number of products manufactured had increased from 25 to 125, and the number of stock-keeping units (SKUs) from 2,000 to 12,000 in the previous three years.

An internal focus had also left me somewhat isolated politically. The corporate environment was changing rapidly and I had not invested time in developing any networks. As the company was a joint venture, inertia between the partners was often evident. It was a 51:49 split. Part of the organizational change reflected this fact. The majority partner controlled the commercial area and the other controlled operations. The change to a regional structure split up operations and gave this partner greater control.

Forsgren and Pahlberg (1992) wrote about the importance of network position in an organization. They contrast it with autonomy and reflect that increased autonomy leaves one badly positioned in terms of network position. Autonomy tends to isolate the subject from the environment. This was an apt description of the issues I faced at that time. A multinational organization is intrinsically a network of units. These units are of varying importance and position. Results are important in maintaining the unit's status but autonomy reduced network position. Reacting to or with the environment was an important factor for any subsidiary. In this type of environment network position is actually more important than autonomy through delivering results. This was an important realization for me at the time. It was to shape my thoughts and opinions over the period in question.

The plant organization became a primary focus for me and the need for greater expertise in distribution was clear. The increasing complexity necessitated a dual focus on manufacturing and distribution. I recruited a logistics manager and began to focus on developing the plant team. I needed to increase the capability of the management team to do their jobs and integrate the plant more into the fabric of the organization. So I set about a collaborative effort at reorganization. I involved the managers in the discussions of how we needed to change and I asked some people at head office for their help in facilitating some of the discussions. This reorganization became central to improvements in the plant's profile and influence at headquarters.

The reorganization was handled as a change programme and I took on the role of the change agent. While it was uncharted territory for me I had considerable back-up support from the MSc programme. The basis I used for change was the structure devised by Beckhard and Harris (1987). The first stage involves developing a defined need for change. This was easy in our environment at the time because it was clear that the plant was lagging in results terms. By working with the team it was easy to highlight the need for change. Everybody accepted that change had to happen.

The second stage is that of developing a desired future state. Once the issues were clear the design of a new structure was the main focus. This activity was where I got people from Florida involved and their facilitation engaged them in the process. Engagement commits people and their involvement committed strong external forces to the overall process. We ended up with a structure, which separated the major production lines and the materials and distribution activities. These activities defined five business units with a set of key measurements for each unit. Leadership was defined and each manager took responsibility for the performance of a specific unit or units. This created a well-defined structure. The simple structure we had used was not conducive to building specific expertise. In the new organization this was addressed by setting up areas of expertise which also had measures defined. These measures were based on developing expertise and consistency in their specific areas.

The third stage defines the present state as a function of the future state. With the clear picture of where we were going this was easily accomplished. The fourth stage maps the transition from present to future. This takes up most time but again is simplified if the future state is easily understood and defined.

Managing during the transition state and institutionalizing the change is the final stage of the process. It is the most difficult to accomplish. Change is not natural for most of us and one tends to revert to old patterns easily. When the units were established we had to make sure that reviews were established to focus the need for results. We educated people on their accountabilities and responsibilities. The commitment of the senior team spawned a new environment in the plant. Results followed and the service difficulties dissipated.

Further initiatives

Buoyed by the success of the reorganization, I started to involve the team in discussions on how we could develop the mandate of the plant. We looked at ways in which we could consolidate the plant's role and ensure our jobs were developing as we moved forward. As we examined our position relative to the environment, it became clear to us that our geographic position in the marketplace was weak and possible threats to the plant came from the possibility of our process being broken up and placed closer to our customers. However, our cost position had improved and we had the benefits of scale on our side. A clear opportunity emerged from an idea to entice customers to set up close to us. This was a development of the practice where suppliers often move close to their customers. If we could encourage this to happen it would leave us well positioned to take advantage. It was another example of developing a desired future state similar to the reorganization example.

With improving performance and relationships with Florida, we had less opposition to moving forward with our idea. It was agreed that I could approach customers with the idea with head office support. They also agreed to fund an incentive to customers in setting up. Within the company it was seen as a well-developed supply-chain initiative with particular relevance to the subcontract-type flow of speciality products. The 'campus concept' format would allow for minimal inventories and faster cycle times. As support grew, the problem became one of making it happen.

One major European customer expressed interest in the idea and we discussed it with them in greater detail. It emerged that with the improved cost position and with some of the financial incentives available in Ireland, it was a good move for them. We entered negotiations with them and agreed a schedule and a financial incentive on our side.

By the end of the MSc programme the company had agreed to push forward with the 'campus concept'. A vacant premises was identified on the same industrial estate and the planning stages began. Unfortunately the company was going through a particularly bad phase at the time and the idea was shelved. In retrospect however, getting the project so far down the road reflected the changing perspective of Optix Ireland. Having recovered from a period of substandard performance, the plant was now pushing the boundaries of its mandate with the support of the corporation.

Reflecting on the campus initiative

Reflecting on the activities of the time it is useful to analyse what was happening then. As a subsidiary of a multinational company, Optix Ireland had a mandate to perform functions within Optix International's global mandate. Thompson (1967) provides a conceptualization of how an organization interacts with its environment and the logic governing these relationships. The domain of an organization, described by Thompson (1967) as its territory, is further clarified by MacKechnie (1995) as the claims which an organization stakes out for itself.

Thompson's concept of domain as an area with boundaries leads us to the logic of interaction with its environment, i.e. external to the boundaries, and we have inputs, which are supplied to the territory and outputs provided from it. The immediate environment provides these interacting bodies and is defined by Thompson (1967) as the task environment.

Dill (1958: 27–28) is quoted by him as defining this task environment as 'those parts of the environment which are relevant or potentially relevant to goal setting and goal attainment . . . those organizations in the environment which make a difference to the organization in question'. These occupy four typical sectors of the task environment:

- customers (both distributors and users)
- suppliers of materials, labour, capital and workspace
- competitors for both markets and resources
- regulatory groups, including government agencies, unions and interfirm associations.

This task environment occupies a part of the overall environment and provides a theoretical construct to define the outside individuals and groups with which the organization interacts. Within the task environment the organization is dependant on these other individuals and groups for supplying inputs and accepting outputs. The dependence relationship may vary due to the level of supply and demand.

The definition of our task environment clearly revolves around the optical device business. The problem emerges when addressing the domain of the organization. As a multinational subsidiary, did we occupy a sub-domain of the corporation's domain or our own domain with inter-company interactions regarded as commitments within the task environment? I have chosen the former, because it best describes the corporate environment. We did not compete with other sites for business. We had a regional supply focus but there was quite an amount of interaction with the organization. As mentioned earlier, network position was important within the corporation.

As we occupied an area of the corporate domain, we hoped to expand our area of occupation. There were two ways of doing this:

- We could extend within the corporate domain and take a larger share of the domain activity, i.e. increase our mandate.
- We could increase the corporate domain and become the pioneers within this extended domain.

The future state we envisaged was the latter of these two. However, we needed to keep an open mind and be prepared for any opportunities, which came our way.

Emerson (1962) wrote about managing dependence upon others by acquiring power over them. He regarded power to be the inverse of dependence. Power stems from the following:

- How much need exists for organizational outputs?
- How many alternatives to these outputs exist?

Basically power is based on needs and alternatives and we could try to improve our position by influencing within the domain or focusing on the task environment. The concept we envisaged involved influencing within the task environment. Consequently we were focusing on the customer (the main element of our task environment) to increase our power within the corporate domain. Our concept seemed to align with the increasing customer focus evident in the corporation. By developing partnerships with our customers we could become a more influential player within the corporation. This could also enhance our prospects of bringing upstream activities to Ireland.

Four basic strategies

Any strategy for Optix Ireland (OI) had to consolidate the business. As per MacKechnie (1995), Emerson's model can be reduced to four basic strategies (see Box 8.1). Within the task environment our target was the customer base. The overall strategy was taking us away from the subcontract supply-chain format to more of a supplier role.

Strategy	Possibilities
Reduce OI's needs of customers	Rationalize OI to focus solely on subcontract manufacture. This would not extend our domain
Increase OI's alternatives to customers	Diversify by increasing brand focus. Go direct to retail
Reduce customers' alternatives to OI	Monopolize by integrating customer activity into Irish activity. Long-term contracts and partnerships
Increase customers' need of OI	Develop the value and felt need of the customers. Increase the benefits to them through enhanced customer focus. More customised service

Box 8.1 Four basic strategies.

This was a key element, which emerged later as an important focus for our strategy. The four generic strategies were as follows. (Note: when I refer to customers I am referring to our direct customers in the supply chain. Strategies referred to as going beyond the customer reflect the integration of their activities and selling to the subsequent stage of the supply chain. This would involve carrying out their activities and possibly competing with them.)

Because our focus on the customer was not as a total domain entity, we were limited in how we could develop some of these strategies. We will develop each option further. A key constraint was that because we operated within the corporate domain it would not be possible for us to pursue some of the options described.

Reduce OI's needs of customers

This strategy would have been impossible as we relied on the customer for the main raw material we used, as well as their custom.

Increase OI's alternatives to customers

This would have meant bypassing our present customers in the business chain. We had relationships and were doing business with most customers in the supply chain. Our company charter, as a joint venture, also limited us to working solely with our direct customers. It was also the case that as a manufacturing plant we did not have the influence to change this.

Reduce customers' alternatives to OI

This option described the future state we envisioned. Our campus concept was focused on increasing the customers' needs of OI. As stated previously, we could not envisage a forward integration step, which would take us into the device finishing business, because of our company charter. There were also problems associated with this because our entry into this area of the business could create tension with other customers even if it was in partnership with a customer. Looking at it from a commitment perspective we would benefit most from a customer setting up on our site. By investing in some of the infrastructure and keeping out of the business of finishing, we could avoid creating an imbalance of relationships among our customers where one customer would become very dependent on us while the others became disenchanted. Setting up on our site would mean a greater commitment from any customer concerned as they would be committing to our location. It would make them more dependent and it would involve less risk and less complexity. We had significant complexity without adding processes. This strategic analysis was an important part of the negotiations.

The campus concept was the key initiative or the core element of this strategy. In summary the type of activities we needed to initiate here were as follows:

- Establish partnership agreement with a customer or customers, to perform finishing operations on our site.
- Improve on-time delivery and increase customer awareness at OI.
- Ensure our cost base allowed us to remain profitable if cost competition were necessary in the region.
- Increase customer linkages and technical support from OI.
- Increase OI's profile with customer base.

Increase customers' need of OI

Here was another area where we could benefit. At present our supply chain was filled with inventory. As we grew the inventory grew. When we added products we experienced obsolescence. But more importantly – our customers experienced it. This, allied with the working capital demands of our expensive products, would make growth difficult for our customers. By streamlining the supply chain and taking on more of the accountability we could make them rely on us more, increasing their needs of us. There was little long-term benefit in the large scale of inventories we carried as our growth demanded more niche and tiered product offerings. It would become an impediment to our growth.

On the contrary if we took control of the supply chain and held more responsibility for it, we could really enhance the customers needs of our service. It could turn a challenge into an opportunity. Initiatives to be pushed here were as follows:

- reduce customer's pipeline inventory;
- increase responsiveness by continual reduction of order lead time;
- improve their profitability;
- manage their speciality product inventory;
- provide a long-term option of physically delivering lenses further down the supply chain while still dealing with them;
- integrate with customers' information systems.

This showed a parallel strategy, which we could develop in order to leverage the benefits of the campus concept. A streamlined supply chain would add to our overall concept of the future creating a bigger brighter picture for us. Obviously these strategies were aimed at the task environment but it was also providing other benefits within our own organization. Developing the initiatives was helping to improve our network position considerably having involved senior figures in the process. This was a secondary benefit of the activity.

Charting the mandate expansion of Optix Ireland

As mentioned in the last section, it was necessary to consolidate the performance of the basic mandate in order to be well positioned to justify investment in expanding the mandate. Birkinshaw and Hood (1998) describe the options open to a subsidiary, both positive and negative, in terms of development. They are:

- parent driven investment
- subsidiary driven charter extension
- subsidiary driven charter reinforcement
- parent driven divestment
- arophy through subsidiary neglect.

Taking a subsidiary's current mandate as a baseline, the change can be positive or negative to that mandate. This effect on mandate can happen through a change in the charter of the subsidiary or through its capability. Birkinshaw and Hood (1998) prescribe two real directional options, i.e. capability and charter both increase or both decrease. Their concept is that whichever moves first pulls the other along, positively or negatively.

Analysing the five options yields the following:

- *Parent driven investment* would be where the parent is investing in the subsidiary of their own volition. It would indicate that the parent saw it as building a competitive advantage. The parent in this case is very committed. This would result in increased capability as the subsidiary takes on more responsibility. The corporate agenda did not have mandate expansion in OI as a priority.
- *Subsidiary driven charter extension* is the long-term direction we wished to take. It describes where the subsidiary manages to extend its capability through different initiatives. The increased capability facilitates an enhancement in charter when opportunities present themselves within the corporation. The subsidiary is ready for such opportunity. Undoubtedly there would also be some political manoeuvrings. Our pursuit of the campus concept for OI was such a strategy.
- *Subsidiary driven charter reinforcement* is the consolidation of the mandate. This is subsidiary driven and it involves the strengthening of the position without improving the capability. This described our first goal and involved strengthening the OI performance against our performance measures.
- *Parent driven divestment* is a loss of charter, which would generally be enacted by the parent. It would result in a reduction of capability, as there would be less activity to maintain the capability. The parent may divest seeing better returns through an alternative investment.
- *Atrophy through subsidiary neglect* – the final option means that the subsidiary loses its capability and consequently its charter typically through lack of focus on the part of the leadership and can end in complete divestment by the parent unless some environmental need saves the subsidiary.

Our long-term goal was subsidiary-driven charter extension. Initially we had to consolidate our position, i.e. subsidiary driven charter reinforcement. Because on-time delivery had become a key measurable, improving our performance here was the priority. We had also needed to address issues of structure, which helped cope with increasing complexity. The reorganization undertaken at the outset had provided charter reinforcement for OI. The campus strategy was one designed to generate charter extension.

Conclusions and reflections

The benefits of action learning revolve around the discipline of reflection on the experience. Here are some of the key lessons I took from the experience.

Is there a right way?

A constantly recurring theme throughout the programme was the idea that problem-solving logic does not always frame an issue. There is not always a correct answer. Johnson (1992) and Dromgoole and Mullins (1999) describe the concept of polarity management. It concerns the need to consider that AND logic is sometimes more relevant than EITHER/OR logic. Polarities are extreme opposite positions and the problem lies in finding the correct balance between both positions. Where the balance lies is very much determined by environmental conditions. An example of this is the question of integration versus responsiveness. At the outset we were very much focused on cost, which aligned with the integrative approach. Then an organizational change and market conditions necessitated a more responsive approach. As we evaluated our strategy it was always a balance we had to strike between both approaches. On one extreme we could focus singularly on cost but it would be detrimental to our responsiveness if we took it to the extreme. If cost is the key factor in the environment then maybe that is the correct course. However it's normally a matter of balance between the two extremes.

To take this further, Box 8.2 shows a polarity map (per Johnson and Dromgoole and Mullins) of integration versus responsiveness.

Higher purpose: develop a low-cost base business as close to the customer as possible finding the balance between cost and growth. Find skillsets more important to the business and not reliant on integration or responsiveness

An integrated business	*A responsive business*
+	–
Greater scale	Proximity to the customer
Better productivity	Reactivity to customer needs
Higher quality	Flexibility
Better efficiency	Entrepreneurial
Increasing specific expertise	General expertise the norm
Systems to combat complexity	High involvement
Cost focus	Growth focus
–	+
Low customer awareness	Increased complexity
Slow to React	Inefficient
Inflexible	Become slave to the customer
Given to bureaucracy	Exposed to low-cost competition
Low value awareness	

Box 8.2 Polarity map of integration versus responsiveness.

This is basically a matrix, which shows the positive and negative attributes of both extremes. On top of the matrix is stated the higher purpose. This defines the balance we pursued. As stated there are positives and negatives associated with both extremes and the balance is dependant on environmental conditions.

Another set of polarities we experienced relates to influence and autonomy. This was an early theme and one of the first key lessons I learned. Network position is associated with the ability to influence. Autonomy, on the other hand, describes a more independent status. It provides for a clearer direction and more efficient operations situation but can lead to isolation. Isolation in a turbulent environment is uncomfortable and in general, network position is extremely important in a multinational corporation. Box 8.3 shows the relevant polarity map. Striking the balance between influence and autonomy was a key part in the struggle for survival and subsequent mandate development at Optix Ireland.

Developing some networking capability was important in finding the correct balance with the environment we occupied. Autonomy had not worked for us.

This led me to examine the nature of finding this balance and relating it back to stages of managerial development. Depending on the environment it is necessary for the manager to alter styles, which is not possible for everyone. However to be an effective leader in a multinational environment it is necessary to bridge these differences. I can best describe this using a 2 × 2

Higher purpose: enough contacts to drive influence on issues while getting the job done

Autonomy	*Networked*
+	–
Get the job done	Wider scope
Fewer variables	Know what's happening
Efficient	Big picture
Know exactly what you are doing	See more opportunities
	More influence
–	+
Limited scope	No defined links
Limited influence	Inefficient
Small picture	Less secure
Not informed	Jobs don't get done

Box 8.3 Influence versus autonomy.

matrix I developed mapping organizational complexity against process complexity. Organizational complexity defines the environment and how dependant the plant is on outside influences. High complexity describes the situation Optix Ireland faced. New plants were coming on stream. The organization was changing focus and growth was a priority. On the opposite scale process complexity defines the internal processes of the plant. As we saw earlier, the need for growth had fuelled a massive increase in the number of products being produced. This had placed a further pressure on the plant. Figure 8.1 shows how I see the management imperatives for striking this balance. While greater autonomy helps to deal with process complexity, network position is called for where organizational complexity is high. Where both are high the manager must truly work to find the balance. It takes both strong management and leadership qualities to survive in such an environment.

Individuals in a multinational environment

One of the greatest difficulties in co-ordinating large organizations is that associated with individuality. I have seen from my experience that teams, far from losing out, are strengthened by individual development. The base unit in any organization is the individual.

Those who write about multi-national corporations tend to predominantly take either a head office perspective or the subsidiary viewpoint. In my opinion this difference in perspective is based on the attitude to the individual. As in my own case, one has to balance the agendas of head office and the subsidiary. One must do what's best for the corporation and also (sometimes foremost) optimize the subsidiary's position.

The irony of the situation is that it is more likely the subsidiary manager who wants to do well for the subsidiary that brings most value to the

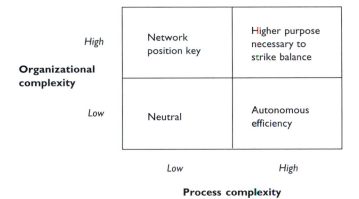

Figure 8.1 Management development matrix.

corporation. Yet the corporate viewpoint would be to mistrust the sub-optimal approach of a subsidiary, even if it generates value for the corporation. Like the issue with teams, groupthink seems far more acceptable within a large organization than individual thought. But highly motivated individuals are more likely to deliver results.

Inordinate value is often placed on international experience within a multinational environment. The focus is often on developing leadership to a global formula. Consequently there is great difficulty in seeing that the dynamic of the individual who runs a subsidiary optimizing for both the subsidiary and the corporation is a powerful force. This is probably what Hedlund (1986) was getting across in his proposal of the multicentred MNC – a heterarchy. In the same way that highly developed individuals make a team stronger, highly developed individuals optimizing subsidiaries will tend to make the corporation stronger. Thus the decentralized approach suggested by Hedlund holds many benefits. It is viewed with trepidation by the people holding the reins in many multinational organizations. But these are the people who stand to lose the control they desire.

References

Beckhard, R. and Harris, R. (1977) *Organizational Transitions: Managing Complex Change*, 1st edition. Addison-Wesley, Reading, MA.

Birkinshaw, J. and Hood, N. (1998) *Multinational Corporate Evolution and Subsidiary Development*. Macmillan, London.

Dill, W. R. (1958) Environment as an Influence on Managerial Autonomy, *Administrative Science Quarterly*, 2: 409–433.

Dromgoole, T. and Mullins, D. (2000) Strategy Implementation and Polarity Management, in P. Flood, T. Dromgoole, S. Carroll and L. Gorman (eds) *Managing Strategy Implementation*. Blackwell, Oxford.

Emerson, R. M. (1962) Power Dependence Relations, *American Sociological Review*, 27: 31–40.

Forsgren, M. and Pahlberg, C. (1992) Subsidiary Influence and Autonomy in International Firms, *Scandinavian International Business Review*, 1(3): 41–51.

Hedlund, G. (1986) The Hyper Modern MNC-A Heterarchy, *Human Resource Management*, 25(1): 9–35.

Johnson, B. (1992) *Polarity Management: Identifying and Managing Unsolvable Problems*. HRD Press, Amherst, MA.

MacKechnie, G. (1995) Managing the Organisation's Environment, University of Dublin Business School Work Paper, Dublin.

Mintzberg, H. (1983) *Structure in Fives, Designing Effective Organizations*. Prentice Hall, Englewood Cliffs, NJ.

Thompson, J. D. (1967) *Organizations in Action*, McGraw-Hill, New York.

Chapter 9

The dominant factors for creating trusting relationships between supervisors and subordinates in a quasi-government agency

Akinyinka O. Akinyele

The state of the mailing industry is one of unlimited opportunities. The work environment as it relates to this quasi-government company is one of fierce competition from different industries. The issues facing this company are competition, product maturity, productivity improvements, attrition of experienced managers and executives, technology, privatization, and on a smaller scale, trust, integrity, accountability, responsibility and transition after the implementation of change.

I grew up under the influence of love and strict discipline. At an early age, it was clear to me that certain values were of major importance to every family member. These values had their base in the Ten Commandments from the Bible. As a child growing up, I found these values becoming clearer each day. They included but are not limited to the following: honesty (do not tell a lie or cheat), integrity (you are believable), fairness (treat everyone right), honour (do not do anything to bring shame to the family name) and education (learn as much as you can).

As I grew up, we were encouraged to stand up for what is right and tell the truth if and when things do not look right. Over the next several years, from elementary through high school, these values were reinforced by the daily interaction with my parents, elders and teachers. It became even clearer during my last year in high school as I had an opportunity to become one of the ten student officers (prefects). We were responsible to oversee and co-ordinate the activities of the student body outside the classroom periods. We also functioned as liaisons between the students, school staff and faculty. I had the opportunity to learn directly from our faculty and administrative staff through daily interactions. It also meant I had to lead by example, doing the right thing every time.

As I continued my life journey, I found that my beliefs in some cases were very helpful and made my interactions very comfortable, while in other instances, I just was not accepted. I was hired as a project engineer with a university system in their physical plant department. I had a manager who was too much involved in office politics for her personal gains. As time went on, through interactions, it became apparent that I had to resolve in written form of communication with her on every single issue. I found myself having a notebook, pen or pencil, whenever we had a conversation. As I reflect on those situations, I realized I had lost complete trust for her based on her interaction with me. I could no longer have open and honest communications with her for fear of her using the information for personal gains. Her actions were no longer aligned with her words. She made decisions that were contrary to what the data suggested without explaining her decision or the reasons for the decision change. On one occasion, during the budget preparation, I had met and discussed all staffing requirements and planned projects with her and each department head. I simulated the figures based on the data and information I had gathered, and presented the draft budget to her prior to the budget meeting. I also consulted with her one-on-one at which time she approved the preliminary budget. At the meeting with department heads, which was less than an hour after my meeting with her, she proceeded to bring up new information. I was stunned and embarrassed, because she did not share the information with me prior to that meeting. Needless to say that situation had a major impact on the final budget and the deadline, I felt rather stupid because of her failure to communicate new changes with me, hence I could not trust her after that.

Upon leaving I was hired as a project engineer with an electronic manufacturing company in 1981; I reported directly to the manager of engineering. Right from the start, he communicated his expectations regarding my performance and behaviour. Being new on the job, I requested to meet with him weekly to discuss my performance and progress. During these sessions, we had open dialogues about our likes and dislikes, about our families and about our visions for the future. Yes, I took a risk to discuss personal issues with him. In the back of my mind, I knew he could discuss my issues with someone else, or use the information against me later in my performance appraisal. He never discussed any of those items with anyone, and I was able to build the trust in him that he would keep confidential issues.

Likewise, he was able to periodically have an open discussion about my performance. My observations of his interaction with other engineers relating to work assignments and performance appraisal led me to the conclusion that he was fair in discharging his duties as a manager. The other aspect of building that trusting relationship was his knowledge of the business. It was critical to me that my supervisor was knowledgeable because I was new in the company and needed more guidance. Because of his knowledge and his willingness to share, he was well respected by all of his subordinates.

As I continued to work in corporate America, I had a desire to find a correlation between my personal belief and what is actually going on in the workplace. During my literature search, I found that there is ongoing discussion of trust in organizations. These discussions have captured the attention of scholars and practitioners such as O'Brien (1995), Ouchi (1981) and Rotter (1971). The authors all agreed on the importance of trust and its role as a critical ingredient of well functioning organizations. In today's competitive environment where there is continuous push for higher perform- ance levels in every organization, trust has come to be revalued as an asset.

This search led me to study the dynamics between supervisors and subordinates within an organization. I conducted the study in quasi- government organization. This organization has embarked on transforming itself; however, the process has been slow and tedious. The facilities in my study are from the Midwest, from the states of Michigan, Illinois and Indiana. The site selection was based on (1) size: number of employee and the volume of products, (2) employee mix, (3) distance from each other and (4) willingness of the management staff to participate in the study. At every site, the research started with an initial meeting with potential participants. During this meeting, the purpose for the research and the follow-up meetings were explained. Before the consent form was distributed, all questions were answered and understanding by everyone present was achieved. Anyone who elected not to participate was excused and the remaining signed a consent form.

As a researcher, I have my own biases that will influence or limit the areas of my research. Building a trusting supervisor–subordinate relationship depends on the participant's beliefs. These beliefs are consciously and unconsciously influenced by the principles and values each person has been exposed to over an entire life. As I have experienced, my beliefs about what is right and wrong are influenced by the values I was brought up with as a child and were enhanced as I became an adult. These beliefs guide my behaviours. Our cumulative behaviours create or destroy a trusting relationship. My personal experiences have continually focused on a few variables for building trusting relationships. These variables are honesty, integrity, fairness, consistency, confidence and knowledge (Figure 9.1).

Although I have spent most of my adult life working for different com- panies, my experiences have been similar regardless of the different cultures within these companies. I have found to be more productive and go the extra mile if and when I feel that there is a trusting relationship between my supervisor and I. As a result of my direct observations and active partici- pation, I will expand through personal examples the impact trust has had on relationships professionally.

In 1992, during a restructuring within my organization, I had an oppor- tunity to consider an individual who will be referred to as Jodi in this story. Jodi was recommended as a candidate with very good administrative skills, but lacking the operational knowledge for the said position. I interviewed her and offered her the position with the understanding that I would depend on her administrative skill in certain situations while she enhanced her operation skills. Later that week she called to discuss new circumstances with her job search. She had been offered another position with a higher salary than the

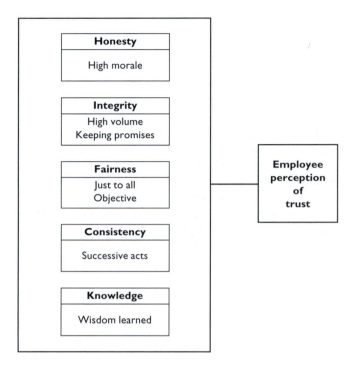

Figure 9.1 Prevailing factors.

one I had offered her. After several minutes of discussion, I wished her well in her new position and asked her to keep in touch. I felt that her openness and willingness to discuss the circumstances personally were courageous and trusting. She took a risk to decline a job offer personally, in an environment where it may have been career suicide. After about one year, I had other job vacancies in my new plant. Some of these positions were the same salary as the one she had earlier accepted in another plant. Jodi called and requested a transfer into one of my positions. I accepted her transfer request and once again offered her a position.

Jodi, along with twelve other managers, reported to me in this newly built processing plant. Over the next several months, she and I developed open, direct and honest communication style. I was able to share pertinent information about our organization with her and other managers as a way keeping them informed. She was constantly communicating with me and other managers. Jodi had high integrity level, and was always honest about everything, even when she knew she might have failed. One day in my absence, she made an operational decision that had a negative outcome to the facility. Upon my return, I had a meeting with her to get a better understanding of the situation before the decision was made. She was forthright about the data and information she had before the decision was made. Over and over she demonstrated her honesty and integrity with numerous and countless situations as a manager for twenty-plus supervisors and as my subordinate.

Earlier in our interaction, she had promised that she would bring two computer systems with her; when she reported to the position she subsequently declined. Jodi during our discussion still offered to send the systems to the facility as she had promised to bring the systems with her. She packaged the systems and sent them to me as discussed. Over and over her behaviour was consistent with her words. She always did what she said she was going to do her actions were always consistent with her words. She can be referred to as 'walking the talk'. Reynolds (1997: 27) wrote, 'Being competent and open is not enough. You have to do what you say you are going to do. People will only trust you if you are reliable, dependable and consistent.' Over time, Jodi had always done what she said she was going to do. She was reliable, dependable and competent, hence, I trusted her to be my primary replacement when I was away from the office.

As I reflect over the years as the plant manager in this facility, I had a very productive facility because the overall trust level between the managers and me and the managers and the employees. Early on in the process it was clear to them that I was ready and willing to accept my responsibility for the performance of the plant. I encouraged the team members to take risks and be innovative in their approach of doing business. Few of the ideas did not work out as well as we thought, however; I accepted the responsibility for the action as well as the result. I communicated the decision to higher-level officers of the company and was willing to accept responsibility for the results. Conversely, I felt Jodi and most of managers trusted me enough to know that my actions would be consistent with my words. The results of having these trusting relationships throughout the facility showed in our performance indicators. Every member of the team, from me down to the machine operators was willing to go that extra mile each and everyday to accomplish the targets of the organization. Our facility was one of top three plants within the region and in the top ten in the nation for four straight years after activation.

Another learning experience for me happened just five short years ago (1998), when I had one of my subordinates who was new to my area of responsibility. Joe was at this time experiencing unacceptable performance. He was in denial because he thought somebody was sabotaging his operation. He started becoming very defensive to the point of bullying his subordinates. The high point came when he decided to tape-record his staff meeting without telling his team members. During the staff meeting, there were some emotions flying around, and some statements made that were unacceptable. After the staff meeting, I ran into one of his subordinates, who proceeded to quote a statement I was supposed to have made. A couple of days later, I received a memo from the group asking for clarity about the possible statement.

I called Joe for a discussion so that I could better understand the context and content of the supposed statement he made during his staff meeting. During this one-on-one meeting, I asked for clarification so that I could be better informed and understand how I would proceed. He shared with me everything but denied the fact that he tape-recorded his staff meeting as he could no longer trust them to follow through on assignments. A few days later, during another discussion he brought up the fact that he had some information on tape that he wanted to share with me. I proceeded to ask him for the source of the information and the setting for the recording. His answer was very upsetting to me because there was conflict with the information he shared with me days earlier. He produced the tape and I asked him about the staff meeting incident. My first thought was to get rid of him immediately; however, I approved one day of leave and asked him to come back. During our follow-up meetings I explained to him how disappointed I was because he had misrepresented the information to me about a week ago. I continued to share with him again my values and beliefs and the importance of integrity and honesty in the workplace. We collectively worked on the damage control with his staff and repairing his relationship with me.

The first step on his damage control action plan was for Joe to have another staff meeting immediately, during which he had to accept responsibility for his actions. He had to apologize to his team members for letting them down and request a new beginning in building a productive team. He asked for comments from the group, who at this time was totally awed and could not believe this was the same person from the last meeting. Joe started sharing more information coming from me to his team members to the point where they thought he was over-communicating. He took time to explain his decisions with the entire plant employees. On occasions when he was not sure of the answer, he felt comfortable saying 'I don't know, however I will research and get you the right answer'. Over the next few months, he started to experience change to his performance results. By the end of that fiscal year, the team was performing very well, but not enough to erase the deficit from the earlier quarters.

Over time, his actions were consistent with his words. I had an opportunity to discuss this incident with him to get his reflective insight of the incident and his journey of rebuilding. He told his group that I have an open and direct communication with my subordinates. He said (and I quote) 'My manager always shares his vision for the cluster. He is always open and direct with each one of us. And he is always willing to take time to explain his decisions.' Joe said he found out he had been wasting his time through not taking time to explain his vision for the group and his decisions. He thought that because he was in charge, his team members would automatically believe him. He also admitted he had not appreciated his members as much as he should. He did not realize that their perception of him was 'one not accepting responsibility' until the tape-recording incident. The team members shared with him examples of times when they were blamed for performance but they were not aware of the targets. He said he started sharing information and whenever in doubt, he accepted the responsibility for not sharing that pertinent information they needed. He himself recognized the dynamics of the team changing, to the point of some members telling him not to accept the responsibility alone since he had shared the information with them, even though they were not successful. Joe said he felt they started to trust him as he stopped blaming them for his mistakes, and he was not withholding any support or behaving in any threatening manner. They even felt comfortable to share confidential information with him, increasing the trust level between him and his staff. During a conversation a year later, he said he learned from those experiences because those things stuck with him over those trying moments. He now understands the value of developing trusting relationship with his subordinates.

Currently I am working with one of my subordinates and his subordinate on a situation that is creating an unhealthy work environment between the manager, supervisors and employees. The preferred style of this management team is one where information is only a directive and those directives should not be questioned. Employees now feel that they are not communicating openly and cannot question what management says. They are being talked to and do not have any input in how the operation is run. They have stated time and again that they are being treated like children. They are not feeling good about coming to work and won't take the initiative to fix anything that is obviously wrong. Moreover, they won't point out to management when something is wrong. They feel that management is on a power trip. One thing the employees know for certain, management cannot do it without them. This tactic of running an operation with an iron-clad fist only alienates the very people you need to make the operation work. This atmospheres fuels poor work performance, employees feel harassed, mistrust and anxiety run rampant and the very core of the workplace environment is threatened on a daily basis. Emotions run high when people feel belittled continuously. An important factor, open communication builds trust, and fosters a feeling of respect. The integrity of the messenger is held in high esteem.

During my intervention, I had a meeting with the manager to discuss how she perceived the working environment. After our discussion, I had the labour officer in with the manager to hear and understand his point of view. It was clear to me that basic communications were missing. The labour officer said, 'If I could know there would be any changes with policy or know beforehand a rule would be enforced then I could discuss this issue with my membership.' Based on my experience and understanding of a trusting relationship, the labour officer was only asking for information sharing.

I have a strong feeling that the working environment will improve once there is open, honest and direct communication between the manager and the labour officer. Sharing of information before things happen explaining decisions without feeling threatened as well as accepting responsibility for their actions. It was also agreed that they would start managing agreements in an effort to improve the interpersonal relationship. Above all, both must act with integrity, and actions must consistent with their words.

Another example is a current subordinate of mine, who feels that because of our open communication, she can disagree without repercussions. This contrasts with a major disappointment she had with her last superior. She now feels good about voicing her opinion and taking responsibility for decisions she is allowed to make as part of her learning process. Moreover, she is thankful for the time we communicate and the 'gift' of a different viewpoint. Her theory is that managers should encourage their subordinates to be vocal in order to leverage their skills. They should welcome dissent and stop entertaining power struggles and the need to control. There should be an active move toward mentoring at all levels, with a team spirit that fosters trust and training. Regardless of one's title, you can learn something from everyone. There should be brainstorming sessions to get input from all departments to track and model successes.

The learning from these actions can be summarized as follows: trusting relationship between supervisor and subordinate is enhanced when all or most of these dimensions are present:

- communication
- integrity
- confidentiality
- responsibility
- consistency.

I have experienced very positive working relationships with my supervisors as well as my subordinates. The main ingredient is an open, direct and honest communication. In each case, an environment of honesty and unquestionable integrity was always present to the point that everyone's energy is directed at being the best. No one felt left out or behaved as not being part of the team. A safe environment was paramount where everyone felt it safe to discuss confidential issues without being for public discussion. An environment where risk is encouraged because everyone was willing to accept responsibility without a doubt.

I have also worked in an environment where I could not trust my supervisor, in an environment where I was guarded and spoke only when spoken to and was very careful about offering new ideas. I personally prefer the positive environment when trust is definitely present. I have experienced this positive environment personally, as a project engineer and as a plant manager. In each case, I enjoyed great accomplishments. As a project engineer, I had high self-esteem and personal self-gratification. I was always willing to go that extra mile. Projects were completed on time with the highest quality. As a plant manager, I enjoyed unprecedented successes. My plant was rated in the top three in the region for every performance indicator.

I have learned that is very crucial to building trusting relationships throughout your organization, if you ever think to have a chance of succeeding. A trusting relationship can be built by practising some basic things:

- have an open direct and honest communication
- have high integrity based on basic values
- be confidential on personal matters
- accept responsibility
- above all, ensure that your actions are consistent with words as well as being consistent over time.

The emerging themes were categorized into 'meaning units' that consist of communication, responsibility, confidentiality, integrity, consistency and emotions and feelings.

In summary, there were common themes found between my personal experiences, the literature review and the participants' findings. These themes are communication, integrity, confidentiality, responsibility and consistency. However, I found that the data collected non-verbal gestures, which provided information on feelings and emotions for the participants. I think that this was a significant finding to be categorized as a theme.

References

O'Brien, R. C. (1995) Employee Involvement in Performance Improvement: A Consideration of Tacit Knowledge, Commitment and Trust, *Employee Relations*, 17(3): 110–120.

Ouchi, W. (1981) *Theory Z*. Addison-Wesley, Reading, MA.

Reynolds, L. (1997) *The Trust Effect: Creating the High Trust, High Performance Organization*. Nicholas Brealey, London.

Rotter, J. B. (1971) Generalized Expectancies for Interpersonal Trust. *American Psychologist*, 26: 443–452.

Part II

Management learning, research and education

Chapter 10

Developing managers not analysts

Action learning based degree programmes for managers

Tony Dromgoole

Programme design principles

In one of many attacks on the MBA as a vehicle for management development, Mintzberg (1989) offered his vision of an alternative:

> My ideal management education would take proven leaders well steeped in . . . one industry and then superimpose on their tacit knowledge and innate intuition the best of skill development, conceptual knowledge, and practical technique, so that they can take a fresh perspective on the very things they know well.
>
> (Mintzberg, 1989: 91)

In the introductory chapter to this book, the features of a programme which might better suit practising managers than the conventional approach were outlined:

- the programme should get close to the manager in his or her job;
- the duration of the programme should be long enough to allow real change to take place or at least show some progress;
- it should be tailored to the participants' needs in the working environment;
- it should allow the learner to have ownership of the learning;
- the learner should learn how to learn;
- learning is fostered by a peer group;
- the learning is greatly enhanced when a real issue is faced rather than a case study of another situation.

In keeping with the earlier discussion, the fundamental principle of a programme for experienced managers is that it should offer a genuine alternative to the conventional MBA format. Therefore from a *process* perspective, an important aspect of the design is to base the programme on action learning rather than traditional lecturing and the case study method.

In an action learning based programme managers are asked to focus primarily on their own live experiences rather than dissecting 'dead bodies', such as case studies of how other managers behaved in other situations (Mumford, 1995). Mumford encapsulates the key features of action learning for managers as follows:

1 Learning for managers and leaders should mean learning to take effective action, not just learning to diagnose a problem.
2 It involves actually taking action, and the risks which go with it.
3 It must involve taking action in relation to an issue which is important or significant to the manager.
4 The manager learns best with and from others in similar situations.
5 In keeping with this , the managers must meet regularly and probe each other's progress.

From this starting point, it follows that such a programme should concentrate on a small group of experienced managers who are willing to share their ideas on the problems they are encountering in their jobs.

To make this work, the programme needs to be centred round the manager in his or her working environment. One way which can be devised to achieve this is to require each participant to initiate a significant change in their area of responsibility, the planning and implementation of which would constitute the centrepiece of the learning experience. The expectation then is that a full range of issues, dilemmas and problems will arise in the course of the change which will provide highly relevant material for individual learning. The programme teaching staff will then provide expert support in dealing with issues as they arise.

Since senior managers find it difficult to leave their jobs for long periods of full-time study, building a programme round a real-life change fits well with a part-time programme. The timetable of the programme also needs to have sufficient flexibility to allow for the pressures on the time of senior managers.

From a *content* perspective, there clearly should be a number of key elements. First, to set the context for change and to focus the change initiative, there should be an analytical phase early on in which the participants get to grips with the current state of affairs. Typically this might include an analysis of the industry or sector the organization operates in; the strategy (implicit or explicit) pursued by the organization; an examination of the way the organization is structured; a look at some of the key behavioural issues – culture and climate, leadership, motivation. This examination would give the participant the opportunity to take and apply relevant models, frameworks and concepts from the management literature to a situation with which they are intimately familiar and allow them see their environment through a new set of lenses. Key issues which require to be addressed would be identified as part of this process.

Second, when formulating an approach to addressing issues highlighted through this analysis the management literature comes into play again. Here the change management and behavioural literature would come into focus. Finally, since the participating manager in such a programme would be engaged in managing change and interacting in various ways with people – whether that be with peers or upwards and downwards in the hierarchy – it is clearly desirable that a portion of the process should engage with self-knowledge and skills in understanding and handling others.

A concrete example of such a programme design in action is the MSc in Management Practice (MPP) which is a joint Irish Management Institute and University of Dublin, Trinity College master's through action learning.

MPP programme design

As outlined in the introductory chapter, this programme was launched in the 1970s. It remains as popular with senior managers as ever and demand for places (which are limited to twelve) usually exceeds the quota. Although a number of changes have been introduced to the structure over the years, the basic principles of the programme design have remained constant. One change has been in the number of participants. As we became more familiar with appropriate teaching material and methods, we gradually increased the class size from four initially to what we now feel is the optimum size of twelve.

The format decided on in the early days was to have two main elements of tuition: first, core seminars on two full days each month in which the group as a whole would cover common material and discuss their progress. The second element was to assign an individual tutor to each participant, costly in time but a way to allow meetings to be arranged at mutually convenient times, if necessary outside normal hours.

Since each participant needed to devise and implement an important change, the programme as a whole fell naturally into two parts. The first part was an orientation phase of six months, during which each participant would give systematic consideration to the problems and opportunities facing the organization. This was to culminate in an orientation paper in which he or she would outline their thinking and decide on a specific intervention. The planning and execution of the intervention would form the substance of the second part of the programme and would finally be written up as a dissertation. The importance of being able to put their experiences and learning in writing was driven on two fronts – the requirement to write a master's thesis but also the assertion by Francis Bacon: 'reading maketh a full man . . . and writing an exact man'.

Some modifications have been made to the programme structure over time. The original two parts of the programme have now been changed to four distinct phases, each around six months in length. Each phase has a clear focus and culminates in a piece of written work (increasing in importance and complexity as the programme develops). The scheme is set out in MacKechnie and Dromgoole (1996) and is reproduced in Table 10.1.

Phase I

The first phase is an orientation phase. The participants armed with some analytical models are required to assess the current status of their organizations. These models cover three main areas. The first grouping deals with the domain of the organization and its positioning in its environment. Models drawn from the power/dependence literature are combined with the more business-oriented strategy models. This group of models are essentially concerned with helping participants to think constructively about *what* activities their organization is engaged in.

The second group of models, dealing with the organizing mode, concern *how* the activities are performed. The centrepiece of this is the input-output system underpinning the value chain. The main focus is on the significance of variations in the complexity of the value chain, which is approached through the structural contingency theory models.

The final group of models, dealing with the integration of the behaviour of individuals in the organization, is drawn from the social psychology literature on culture, rewards, group dynamics and the importance of values – in essence offering an explanation of *why* an organization's members should choose to engage in the specific pattern of activities. Readings on culture,

Table 10.1 Phases in action learning based master's programmes for senior managers

Timing	Focus of material	Completion exercise
Months 1–5	*Phase 1* Apply basic strategy, design and behavioural models to own working situation	Brief orientation paper based on models given
Months 6–10	*Phase 2* Elaborate basic models in order to identify key issues and select appropriate areas of intervention	Dissertation proposal (verbal and written)
Months 11–16	*Phase 3* Extended reading on selected topics and development/progress of physical intervention	Position paper (written)
Months 16–24	*Phase 4* Completion of intervention, analysis of results, assessment of learning points	Dissertation draft (verbal and written)

Source: adapted from MacKechnie and Dromgoole (1996).

leadership, reward systems and power and influence are all generally found by participants to be particularly helpful.

These three groups of models are studied and applied during the first five months of the programme and are discussed in the two-day seminars in that first phase. They have proven useful for the participants to address the basic question of the orientation phase, 'Where are we now?', and provide a framework for the written orientation paper which completes the first module. The models provide a foundation and further theoretical material is added as the programme progresses.

The orientation paper, usually some 10,000 words in length, serves to crystallize the participant's views. With the help of some coaching from the tutor, the participant gets experience in reflecting on ideas from the literature and applying them to the concrete circumstances of his or her own job. A second member of the tutor group is asked to make a written comment pointing out both strengths and weaknesses but with an emphasis on constructive criticism.

Phase 2

The purpose of the second phase is to move from the static analysis of the orientation paper to a consideration of where and how a strategic change might usefully be initiated. Broad areas of weakness or opportunity will often have been identified in the orientation phase: the organization might be suffering from a loss of market power or a structural misfit; alternatively, it might be well placed to benefit from a technological advance or a product innovation.

Participants are encouraged, with the support of their tutor and the help provided by class discussion, to identify a broad objective and look in more detail at relevant management literature. The group as a whole spends time studying and discussing selected literature on the management of change. This module finishes with a dissertation proposal. Each participant makes a presentation to the full class and a group of the tutors. The free discussion which follows each presentation is taped and used by the participant to refine his or her ideas before submitting a written proposal of about 10,000 words.

Phase 3

Once the dissertation proposals are settled, various experts are invited to give the participants a brief introduction to specialized management topics, such as human resource management, information systems, operations management or strategic marketing. These are not dealt with as areas of substantive learning, as in courses on an MBA programme. The aim is rather to make the participants aware of areas of literature that might turn out to be relevant to the intervention they are planning.

A second important element of this phase is the early focus on self-knowledge and dealing with others. Various instruments are used and a process has been designed to achieve this in as non-threatening a way as possible.

To 'encourage' reading beyond the core which is relevant to their specific area of intervention, each participant must submit a focused literature review. Typically these reviews are 7,000 to 10,000 words.

With these sources of guidance, and with advice from his or her personal tutor, the participant gets to grips with the practicalities of the intervention. Participants are asked to write a position paper to ensure that they are paying due attention to making sense of the events they are engaged in – acting and reflecting rather than merely acting. Typically this is a skeleton of the thesis.

Phase 4

The final phase is spent in bringing the intervention to a conclusion, analysing and reviewing the results, reflecting on the learning points and writing up the final dissertation. During this phase, the members of the group continue to meet monthly to swap notes. They also spend more and more time with their tutors. Considerable coaching is normally required since the dissertation is usually about 45,000 words and few of them have written a document of this length before. The dissertation itself is often a fairly complex document, combining a narrative with a discussion of a range of issues and contextual background.

Each participant is expected to produce a first draft of the dissertation two months before final submission and give an oral presentation to the group and selected tutors. The feedback two months before final submission gives time to take account of suggestions and criticisms made at the presentation and for any other refinements to be made to the draft.

Behavioural underpinnings of MPP

Adapted from Dromgoole and Gorman (2000), some of the reasons why an action learning based programme along the lines described can be effective are outlined in this section.

The analysis which spurs the change initiative in the first phase is carried out by and therefore *owned* by the participant, *not* by consultants or any other person. Ownership of the diagnosis is strongly recommended by the change management and counselling literature (e.g. Nelson-Jones, 1997; Bennis *et al.*, 1976). The impact of ownership of the diagnosis is powerfully illustrated in Derek Whelan's chapter in this book.

The fact that participants see a programme as relevant to their personal and organizational needs is very important. Cynthia Deane's chapter is worth reading in this respect. An important issue for adult learners is that they perceive the relevance to important goals they wish to pursue. The literature on andragogy, the science of adult learning, emphasizes the importance of perceived relevance (Knowles *et al.*, 1985).

Bandura (1977) and others writing on social learning emphasize the importance to people of credible and prestigious models in advancing change. The fact that the feedback participants receive comes from peers and sources they would regard as prestigious within the group make it very acceptable and influential. Although it is not covered in his chapter, Derek Whelan benefited greatly from advice in relation to a particular capital investment from a prestigious peer on MPP. He didn't make the investment and reaped the benefits.

'Saying is believing' is a phrase which helps characterize the escalating commitment which is part and parcel of the regular presentations made to peers on programmes of this nature – for example, the monthly presentations where participants announce their intention to take certain actions. The regular public commitment to certain actions adds an additional push to the desire to see these actions through so as not to appear inconsistent. This is an example of cognitive dissonance at work (Aronson, 1995).

The intolerance of 'waffle' in the class by fellow participants forces individuals to be more specific on goals, which in turn has a major impact on motivating them to achieve these goals – goal theory at work (Latham and Locke, 1979).

We know from counselling psychology and learning that situations which are psychologically safe, that is free from ridicule or arbitrary evaluation, and with a strong emphasis on the creation of a positive climate, lead individuals to review their behaviour with a view to creating new visions of alternative ways of behaving. Such a climate is good for 'unfreezing' (Lewin, 1951) individuals' present behaviour and enables alternative actions to be considered, planned for and hopefully executed. After some months high trust levels with high degrees of psychological safety are created in the group on programmes such as these. This process can be expedited in some groups by the openness modelled by individual class members who encourage others to feel that it is safe to be open. Thus a high degree of openness and trust can be created in each class which leads members to voice aspirations, fears and doubts which would not surface in a lower trust group. If these ambitions and anxieties are not surfaced the group ends up interacting on and discussing much more superficial issues than those they really require to discuss – the real issues of many of the businesses.

While the climate of the classroom is supportive and psychologically safe it is not 'pollyannaish' in atmosphere. Feedback is sought and given by participants to each other. This feedback was once described by one participant as 'sympathetic confrontation'. So the atmosphere is more 'tough love' than 'love in' and, as another participant said, 'there was no place to hide'. Coaching by tutors and programme leaders is characterized by the same approach. While it is supportive it is not a collusive joining of the participants and staff in a self-delusionary process. In relation to action learning and learning organizations, this is a very important point. And it is connected with the phenomenon of learning or the illusion of learning from experience, specifically failure. There is research evidence that people who work as performing artists and athletes often become obsessed with their performance failures, constantly reviewing video playbacks of the events in order to isolate faults. In contrast, the research shows that business people appear to practise avoidance. They say they keep themselves too busy to spend time reflecting on negative outcomes. So, while we are inclined to say that there is more to be learned from failure than success, it is not as simple as that. When business people fail, there are numerous examples of the unusual lengths they go to, to restore their sense of being able to avoid failure the next time. We need to scrutinize claims by individuals or groups to have learned from failure. When this 'learning' becomes a desperate attempt to escape bad feelings, it may accomplish that goal without producing lessons which actually prevent reoccurrence. Studies show that business people (especially men) are uncomfortable with emotion charged situations. In their haste to move out of the emotional discomfort zone generated by an embarrassing failure, business decision makers may opt for a 'quick-fix' plan that does not address the root problem. In part at least, this may explain the prevalence of single loop learning in organizations where one might expect to see evidence of double loop learning. Single loop solutions (see Senge, 1990) deliver a 'feel good' factor more rapidly than double loop, giving managers the comforting illusion that something is being done to solve the problem (Langer, 1983; Argyris, 1990, 1992). It is reasonable to contend that in the conduct of action learning based master's programmes, the conditions pertaining and the atmosphere of 'tough love' as referred to above reduces the chances of single loop learning taking root.

In MPP there is an important section devoted to 'self-knowledge'. The relevant framework of relevance to programme design here is derived from gestalt therapy (Beisser, 1970) – the paradoxical theory of change. The basic idea here is that individuals and systems change when they confront and know their own behaviour and its impact. So the focus should be not the past or the future. It is what is happening in the present. The paradoxical element here is that change will occur if the realities of the present are fully confronted. An example of this point of view in action is the power of closed-circuit television (CCTV) to change individual behaviour. When we see ourselves on CCTV, it does not tell us how we *ought* to behave, it shows us how we *do* behave. This revelation typically leads to a powerful desire to change our behaviour because we see what that behaviour is and we judge what its impact is. Thus a full confrontation with reality often leads to a diagnosis of how we need to change if our impact is to be more satisfactory – from our own point of view and in relation to our own goals.

Participants and their interventions on the MSc in Management Practice

Participants come from a wide range of managerial backgrounds. The strongest single source has been senior managers of multinational sub-sidiaries – 45 per cent of our graduates. Other important sources are large domestic firms (30 per cent), small entrepreneurial firms (16 per cent) and a small but increasing number from the public service (7 per cent). Just over 80 per cent of participants are between 35 and 45 years of age, with a mean of 39 years – almost exactly ten years older than post-experience MBA students.

Patterns have emerged of common issues that participants have chosen to address in their dissertations both on the MPP and the other programmes represented in this book. Managers from multinationals frequently seek to adopt strategies to improve both the corporate situation as well as that of the subsidiary. A good example of this is Paddy McDermott's chapter. Well-established firms are often wrestling with problems of restructuring and innovating – in some cases the intervention concerns initiating this sort of reform. A case in point is the story told in the chapters by Thomas Schmidt and by Cynthia Deane. In other cases the focus is on dealing with the operational and supply chain issues. For small firms, some of the most common preoccupations are: coping with the problems that arise at the end of the initial growth phase; establishing a rationale to determine the most appropriate form of growth; and coping with the unique circumstances in the family firm. Frequently managers participating in this programme use the opportunity to test the effectiveness of widely used techniques and approaches which are in vogue. Cynthia Deane's use of learning networks in a concrete and real organizational setting is a good example.

Assessing the educational role of the programme

The behavioural underpinnings have been outlined earlier The distinctive feature of the programme is that the participants learn from the concrete problems and opportunities facing them and their organizations. One advantage of this is they are, by definition, working on issues of real, immediate relevance rather than issues assumed to be important by the writer of a textbook or the designer of a syllabus. Second, the participants are forced to evaluate the usefulness of the theoretical models and propositions that they encounter – they rapidly discover whether attractive ideas actually stand the test of real-life circumstances. Third, this form of learning is more likely to have an enduring impact, particularly when participants know that they will have to live with the consequences of their actions.

The trade-off is that the programme has a very specific focus on the issues which turn out to be relevant to the intervention. This does not mean that the focus is excessively narrow – on the contrary, a considerable range of activities are normally involved in devising, planning and implementing an important initiative. However, a conventional MBA or similar programme usually covers a wider repertoire of managerial skills, and cover them in a more systematic fashion. A programme such as the MPP should probably not be regarded as a substitute for an MBA, which is principally intended to provide a broad foundation for managers at a reasonably early stage in their careers. The MPP sacrifices this in favour of attempting to deepen the participants' understanding of the subtleties of the processes they are involved in as managers.

At its best, this kind of action learning programme gives a richer learning experience than orthodox programmes. It reinforces the benefits of co-operation, rather than competition, between participants. It stresses the virtues of learning by reflecting, by acting, by talking, and by listening to the views of peers. It forces participants to do more than follow ideas from the management literature and explain them in exams; they need to gain a thorough understanding of the ideas they wish to use if they are going to apply them to the practicalities of their jobs. It also forces them to articulate their learning and express their thoughts in relatively long and complex written work – a valuable antidote to the attachment to pure action found in much management ideology.

It has become clear from observing a wide variety of participants that some gain far more from the programme than others. Those who benefit most seem to have some characteristics in common. They are self-starters who quickly develop a sense of 'ownership' over what they are doing, and apply their own standards of success rather than aiming at the expectations of the staff or fellow students. As well as sufficient intellectual capacity to absorb some fairly difficult ideas, they have disciplined minds and are prepared to think these ideas through with some rigour. They have enough seniority to be able to embark on a worthwhile intervention, and the courage to take the risks which will almost certainly be involved. Above all, they have a quality which we have come to call 'authenticity' – a propensity to address the all the problems and ideas they come across without fear or favour, and to learn from their own mistakes and prejudices rather than seek to suppress or deny them.

However, there are hazards for some participants. For example, each participant is ultimately responsible for deciding the nature of the intervention and it is easy to fail to develop a sufficiently clear sense of direction. Again, the familiar difficulties of the participant observer can result in the participant getting too close to the events he or she is trying to learn from. It is also clear that some individuals do not always succeed in applying theoretical models effectively, and often do not manage to reflect accurately the events they describe. These factors can undermine the learning intentions of the progranune.

On balance, we have found that the majority of graduates look back on the programme as a valuable learning experience – indeed, there are some who give it the credit for transforming their management career. The MPP has provided us with the opportunity to bring together the two traditions: research, respect for theory and academic rigour from the university; a focus on the problems of practice, skills in adult education and rapport with the business community from the management institute. In particular the MPP has confirmed to us that the dichotomy between theory and practice is a false one.

References

Argyris, C. (1990) *Overcoming Organizational Defenses: Facilitating Organization Learning*. Allyn and Bacon, Boston, MA.

Argyris, C. (1992) *On Organizational Learning*. Blackwell, Oxford.

Argyris, C. and Schön, D. (1978) *Organizational Learning: A Theory of Action Perspective*. Addison-Wesley, Reading, MA.

Aronson, E. (1995) *The Social Animal*, 6th edition. Freeman, New York.

Bandura, A. (1977) *Social Learning Theory*. Prentice Hall, Englewood Cliffs, NJ.

Beisser, A. (1970) The Paradoxical Theory of Change, in J. Fagan and I. Shepherd (eds) *Gestalt Therapy Now*. Science and Behavior Books, Palo Alto, CA.

Bennis, W. G., Benne, K. D., Chin, R. and Corey, K. E. (1976) *The Planning of Change*, 3rd edition. Holt, Rinehart and Winston, New York.

Dromgoole, T. and Gorman, L. (2000) Developing and Implementing Strategy through Learning Networks, in P. Flood, T. Dromgoole, S. Carroll and L. Gorman, *Managing Strategy Implementation*. Blackwell, Oxford.

Knowles, M. S. and Associates (1985) *Andragogy in Action*. Jossey-Bass, San Francisco, CA.

Langer, E. J. (1983) *The Psychology of Control*. Sage, Thousand Oaks, CA.

Latham, G.P. and Locke, E. (1979) Goal Setting: A Motivational Technique that Works, *Organizational Dynamics*, Autumn: 69–80.

Lewin, K. (1951) *Field Theory in Social Science*. Harper and Row, New York.

MacKechnie, G. and Dromgoole, T. (1996) An Action Learning Programme for Senior Managers, Paper delivered to the Mid-Career University Education Workshop, Copenhagen Business School, Copenhagen.

Mintzberg, H. (1989) *Mintzberg on Management*. Macmillan, New York.

Mumford, A. (1995) Learning in Action, *Industrial and Commercial Training*, 27(8): 36–40.

Nelson-Jones, R. (1997) *Practical Counselling and Helping Skills*. Cassell, London.

Senge, P. (1990) *The Fifth Discipline: The Art and Practice of the Learning Organization*. Doubleday, New York.

Chapter 11

Managers' learnings in action

The scholar-practitioner, organization development and action research

Peter Sorensen

This chapter draws on the contributions by the reflective managers presented in the other chapters of the book. Although it represents the integration of various contributions, it draws primarily from three of the authors, Mary Lou Kotecki, Akinyinka O. Akinyele and William J. Kohley. The reason that this chapter is based more heavily on these authors is simply because I am more familiar with their work, each having received their PhD from the Benedictine University PhD programme. I have had the opportunity to get to know and work with each of the authors over an extended period of time. In fact, I had the privilege of working with Akinyinka Akinyele on an award-winning organizational change project.

The chapter also draws on the work of the senior editor of this book, David Coghlan (2001). The chapter employs the contribution of the Benedictine University scholars and the work of Coghlan as an opportunity to review and explore emerging current work and trends in the field of organization development and change.

The chapter deals primarily with four topics. The first topic deals with the idea of the scholar-practitioner, a concept that in a number of ways is related to the concept of the reflective manager. The discussion focuses on trends in education dealing with the scholar-practitioner and the role of the scholar-practitioner in contributing to both the development and the application of knowledge in the field of management and organization development.

The second topic deals with the field of organization development and its primary research methodology – action research. This discussion includes a review of the most recent development in action research, the topic of appreciative inquiry. One of the reasons for selecting appreciative inquiry as an illustration of current versions of action research is that it has been cited in a survey of the world's most influential members of the OD field as the most important current innovation in this field (Warrick, 2002).

The third topic deals with the question of doing action research in your own organization – an activity which is frequently practised by the reflective manager and OD scholar-practitioner. Illustrations are drawn from material presented by the Benedictine University scholar-practitioners and the work of David Coghlan (Coghlan and Brannick, 2001). This section builds on and extends the model presented by Coghlan.

The final section provides a brief summary and personal reflections pertaining to the education of the scholar-practitioner, the reflective manager and the development and practice of knowledge related to OD and organizational change.

The evolution and emergence of the role of the scholar-practitioner

The role of the scholar-practitioner is not a new concept but it is a concept which is receiving increasingly more attention. It is a concept that is directly relevant to the discussion of the reflective manager. In many ways the reflective manager concept is a part of the scholar-practitioner concept and in some ways is a prerequisite for the role of the scholar-practitioner.

The search for ways of bringing the world's and contribution of the scholar and the practitioner together has long been with us. Each has a unique understanding of the world of management and organization. The potential contribution of combining these two contributions offer the promise of significant gains in our knowledge of management and organizations and a significant contribution to increased performance.

The scholar provides the thoughtful reflective integration of data and themes into new or more refined ways of conceptualizing and thinking about the topic of organizations. The scholar has the responsibility for creating generalized models of understanding. The practitioner on the other hand plays a more concrete role and is responsible for the implementation and practice of knowledge. Each role has its contribution and limitations. The scholar has the disadvantage of being removed from the action world, has the problem of acquiring data or organization access as well as the problem of acquiring 'real' knowledge due to the inability to comprehend the complexities of the environment in which the data are being collected (Gummesson, 2000).

The practitioner on the other hand may not be familiar with current models and thinking available more readily to the scholar.

The role of the scholar-practitioner has been receiving considerably greater attention in recent years. The scholar-practitioner refers to a range of practitioner roles. In the field of organization development and management it refers most frequently to managers, human resources personnel, and OD consultants both internal and external. It usually refers to a person who has received advanced education, at the master's or doctoral level in the field. It refers to a person who identifies with and perceives themselves as serving as a scholar-practitioner.

The scholar-practitioner is a person who through this formal education is familiar with the literature, models and theories in the field and is well versed in the methodologies of knowledge development particularly action research. The scholar-practitioner is also that person who ideally has a successful career as a practitioner with immediate and first-hand knowledge of the working of organizations.

The concept of the scholar-practitioner has its roots in an ongoing discussion of research and knowledge which is relevant to practice (Lawler *et al.*, 1985). Bennis appropriately describes the creation of meaningful research as dependent on high levels of collaboration between the research and the client (Lawler, 1985). The scholar-practitioner potentially serves several roles in facilitating meaningful research.

First, the scholar-practitioner serves as a link between the researcher and the organization. As a member of both cultures the practitioner-scholar is able to translate and create meaning between the two cultures. The scholar-practitioner has an appreciation of the norms, appropriate behaviour and values embodied in both. The scholar-practitioner can provide entry and road maps to navigate the complexities and subtleties of the organization.

Second, the scholar-practitioner has the capability of serving as her or his own action researcher within his or her own organization. Education for the action researcher has been part of master's level education in the field of OD since the late 1960s, while more recently the scholar-practitioner has received significantly more attention at the doctoral level. By way of illustration, the Organization Development and Change Division of the Academy of Management in the United States has recently created a doctoral consortium for doctoral students in scholar-practitioner doctoral programmes. Within three years the number of schools and programmes increased from six to eighteen international programmes including such schools as Nottingham University (UK), Case Western Reserve University (US), George Washington University (US), Benedictine University (US), The Fenix Programme at the Stockholm School of Economics (Sweden), Alliant International (US) and Pepperdine University (US), among others. The scholarly productivity of these programmes is well illustrated by the contributions to this book and, for example, a recent publication from the Swedish Fenix Programme (Adler *et al.*, 2004).

In discussing the role of the scholar-practitioner, one particularly helpful way of understanding this role is the work of Gummesson (2000), who develops the notion of 'pre-understanding'. Pre-understanding refers to insights or knowledge of a problem prior to research or problem exploration. Gummesson makes the point that pre-understanding on the part of academics or scholars is based on formal knowledge, while the consultant or manager's pre-understanding is based on experience. Pre-understanding based on *both* sources, formal knowledge *and* experience, places the scholar-practitioner in a highly favourable position in terms of both contribution to knowledge and to its application. Mary Lou Kotecki, William Kohley and

Akinyinka Akinyele provide illustrations of the role of both formal knowledge and experience.

Organization development and action research

Organization development has its roots in the turbulence of the 1940s and has evolved into an applied behavioural science based discipline concerned with the management of organizational change. It has become a complex set of strategies and knowledge related to the area of change and is practised on a global basis (Sorensen *et al.*, 2003).

Central to the early development of the field was the work of Kurt Lewin (Weisbord, 1987), who set forth the early principles and applications of what has become the central research methodology in the field – action research.

Although there are a number of variations of the action research model, core characteristics central to most definitions of action research include the following (based on Cummings and Worley, 2000):

- It is iterative and ongoing in nature. That is, it involves a cyclical process, which continuously reviews and incorporates learning into organizational change projects.
- It is collaborative. This is one of the fundamental characteristics in that it requires high levels of collaboration between the organization development practitioner and members of the organization.
- It contributes to both the learning about and implementation of change to specific situations.
- It also has as its objective, contribution to the larger body of systematic knowledge development concerning organizational change.

Action research has an extensive history involving significant work in the United States, the United Kingdom, particularly at the Tavistock Institute, London, and the Scandinavian countries characterized by the Norwegian Industrial Democracy Project, as well as other areas of the world.

Action research is an area that appears to be particularly well suited for the scholar-practitioner, a role which draws on and contributes to the field's more generalized formal knowledge in relationship to specific situations related to organizational change. In fact, several of the contributors make reference to the application of a more recent and increasingly popular approach to action research known as appreciative inquiry.

Again, appreciative inquiry appears to be particularly appropriate for the scholar-practitioner. Appreciative inquiry relates to each of the central topics of the chapter – action research, the scholar-practitioner, and the process of doing research as a manager in your own organization.

Appreciative inquiry (AI) is specifically referred to by Mary Lou Kotecki in terms of her change project within her organization, and by William Kohley in his survey project. Akinyele, although he does not make specific reference to AI nevertheless has been heavily involved in the use of AI and in fact is the initiator of an award-winning AI project undertaken within his organization, Outstanding OD Project of the Year Worldwide 1997, from the Organization Development Institute. His award-winning work also serves as the basis for understanding how one effectively implements appreciative inquiry as an action research project as a manager in one's own organization.

AI was initially set forth as an adaptation of action research and provides an approach to action research very much within the Lewinian tradition. It is directed toward the creation of positive change and is the product of work undertaken at Case Western Reserve University in the early 1980s and is most clearly associated with the work of David Cooperrider (Cooperrider and Srivastva, 1987).

Since the late 1970s, AI has become a worldwide phenomenon (Sorensen *et al.*, 2003). Contrasted with traditional organizational change that is described as problem-oriented or deficit based change, appreciative inquiry is characterized by the identification of an organization's positive core as the basis for the creation of a desired future state and catalyst for change. In brief, the AI process includes the selection of affirmative topics; the discovery of what is best about the organization, and processes for using positive characteristics or strengths as the foundation for positive change. Although AI has been applied across a number of different areas of organization change, small groups, intergroups, community development and global transformation (Whitney and Trosten-Bloom, 2003) its most frequent application is consistent with what has been described as pragmatic action research (Greenwood and Levin, 1998). Appreciative inquiry has much in common with pragmatic action research, which is described as providing arenas for dialogue, the sharing of experiences, and application of a variety of behavioural science processes.

What is now the most frequently used AI intervention is the AI Summit and the four-dimensional process of discovery, dream, design and destiny, based on the creation of dialogue formed by shared common positive experiences. The AI Summit in fact has much in common with other pragmatic action research approaches such as search conferences and other large group methodologies focusing on creating a shared history, a shared vision and the creation and implementation of actions plans (Janoff and Weisbord, 1992).

One of the more recent applications is the integration of appreciative inquiry with one of the oldest forms of action research, databased change or survey feedback, as presented and discussed in the chapter by William Kohley. In this application of appreciative inquiry and survey feedback, organization members are asked to reflect on peak experiences within their organization and to describe the organizational characteristics or culture associated with these peak experiences.

Work with this integrated AI survey feedback approach to action research has resulted in contributions to both knowledge, understanding and application to specific situations as well as the more general knowledge of change. Applications have been made in a variety of organizations internationally (Sharkey and Sorensen, 2002).

This work has provided a number of additional insights pertaining to organizational change, which includes the concept of a 'latent positive culture', and offers the possibility of a new alternative to change management.

A second contribution to our knowledge of organizational change is an understanding of the organizational characteristics of 'peak experience'. An ongoing analysis of respondents' descriptions of peak experiences from vastly different organizations in the United States, Europe and Asia indicates that peak organizational experiences are characterized by times of high task accomplishment under difficult conditions with high degrees of collaboration.

Each of the three contributors – Mary Lou Kotecki, William Kohley and Akinyinka Akinyele – among the other contributors illustrate the potential and actual contributions to be made by the reflective manager in their role as scholar-practitioners and action researchers.

The process of action research – extending the model

Previous portions of the chapter focused on the role and potential of the reflective manager in terms of contribution to knowledge in the field of organization development through the role of the scholar-practitioner and action researcher. This portion of the chapter focuses on the qualities of the action researcher in terms of doing action research within their own organization. Basically it presents an extension of the model so well developed in the pioneering and classic work on the subject by Coghlan and Brannick (2001).

Coghlan and Brannick (2001) set forth a series of considerations. They refer to the insider change agent as the 'irreverent inmate'. Their discussion of political strategy draws on the work of Buchanan and Boddy (1992) who define the political role in terms of 'performing' – managing the change process and backstaging – which is defined as a political process. They also build on the work of Greiner and Schein (1988) in terms of ten power relationships including relationships with the sponsor, the sponsor's relationship with other executives, the relationship of executives with each other, the relationship between the researcher and significant others, the relationship between the sponsor and other executives, between executives and others in higher management, executives and organizational members, independent mutual relations, subordinates, customers and clients, and with peers.

This discussion builds on and extends the Coghlan and Brannick (2001) model defining the political aspect of action research in one's own organization. The discussion includes six additional concepts which include the idea of aggressive fit, understanding the culture, value orientation, credibility, building networks and evaluation of change.

The discussion again draws on experiences and observations based on the work of Mary Lou Kotecki, William Kohley and Akinyinka Akinyele. Each of the three represents notable illustrations of each of the six concepts.

- *Aggressive fit*: this concept is consistent with Coghlan and Brannick's (2001) definition of the insider change agent as the 'irreverent inmate', someone who supports the organization members, but questions and challenges some of the organization rituals and beliefs. Aggressive fit refers to a person within the organization who fits the general culture, norms and expectations but in a manner which aggressively works at challenging and modifying those aspects of the culture, norms and expectations which inhibit the potential of the organization – a person who is sensitive to the margin or boundaries of deviant but still acceptable behaviour.
- *Understanding the culture*: this concept is essential to the aggressive fit concept. Each of the cited contributors was a successful, long-term, senior member of their organization. In addition, each had received extensive formal education in organization development concepts and was familiar with the literature as well as instruments and measures pertaining to organization culture. Each of the contributors demonstrated a high level of sensitivity to their cultural environment and was well suited to the idea of 'aggressive fit'.
- *Value orientation*: members of the field of organization development share a set of values that define the field. These values include an orientation towards high membership involvement and participation, openness and organizational change which is collaborative and which benefits both the individual member and the total organization.
- *Credibility*: each of the contributors had established credibility within their organization through years of success within their organization. Each had demonstrated a commitment to work through difficult times and different situations in a manner that was consistently beneficial to the organization. Each had established a track record of success, success that included different change situations. Each had established in their own organization a high level of credibility not just with their colleagues and fellow executives but also with members at all levels of the organization. Akinyinka Akinyele, in particular, had established a national reputation as a 'turnaround' and change specialist, and champion of all members in the organization. Again, Akinyele has been able to establish on the basis of his track records and reputation, new and ongoing major action research projects. His chapter on the role and importance of establishing trust is a major factor in determining his level of credibility

and continuing work with the support of members throughout all levels of the organization.

- *Building networks*: all six of the concepts are interrelated and critical to successfully establishing and maintaining a political environment and relationship supporting action research activities. Each of the contributors was noted for investing in networks across departmental and hierarchical boundaries. Each of the three contributions invested considerable time in establishing networks based on trust, values around openness and involvement, maintaining credibility within the context of an understanding and appropriately changing the existing organizational culture.

- *Evaluation of change*: an additional role for the internal scholar-practitioner is the 'evaluator of change' to the extent that the scholar-practitioner serves as a bridge between external researchers and consultants, and the organization. The role of evaluator of change refers to the need to access organization development and change efforts not only in terms of their viability but equally important, their necessity. Advocates of organization development and action research are by their calling, advocates of change and that change is necessary and good, when that is clearly not always the case. There is a growing interest in the value of continuity and stability illustrated by issues and comments made by Lyman W. Porter as part of the 1983 Conference on research sponsored by the Center for Effective Organization and the School of Business Administration of the University of Southern California (Lawler *et al.*, 1985).

Similar comments were reflected in 2001 in an award-winning paper at the Academy of Management by a group of Norwegian organizational scholars (Stensaker *et al.*, 2001).

An increasing number of articles and books are concerned with the unanticipated negative consequences of change such as Wayne F. Cascio's (1993) article 'Downsizing: What Do We Do Now? What Have We Learned?', which describes the negative consequences of downsizing, and Eliezer Geisler's (1997) book *Managing the Aftermath of Radical Corporate Change*, which identifies the problems related with radical change and strategies for healing and reconstruction.

Personal reflection

Most of my professional career has involved both the practice and education in the field of organization development and change. I was fortunate to have my first experience in the field as an internal, organizational member of an organizational analysis department, which served as a host to a number of researchers from area universities such as the University of Chicago and the University of Michigan. There I had the opportunity to experience the role of both the scholar-researcher and the practitioner. In some ways it was trial-by-fire as I learned of the difficulties of trying to provide guidance and assistance to academic researchers familiar with the literature that served as the basis for their research. I experienced the vulnerability of young PhD candidates attempting to do research in complex corporate cultures which were not necessarily always receptive to the jargon and perceived naive world of the academics.

I experienced the invaluable contribution of executives who were familiar with and comfortable in both the academic and corporate world. I had the opportunity to experience first hand the role of credibility, trust, knowledge of the culture, networking and pre-understanding based in both formal knowledge and experience.

My role more recently has involved scholar-practitioner education at the PhD level, working with exceptional practitioners making the transitions to the scholar side of the scholar-practitioner. My experience has been that the scholar-practitioner represents an increasingly important and viable role in bridging two sometimes very different but mutually dependent cultures.

References

Adler, N., Shani, A. and Styhre, A. (eds) (2004) *Collaborative Research in Organizations: Foundations for Learning, Change and Theoretical Development.* Sage, Thousand Oaks, CA.

Buchanan, D. and Boddy, D. (1992) *The Expertise of the Change Agent.* Prentice Hall, London.

Cascio, W. (1993) Downsizing: What Do We Do Now? What Have We Learned? *Academy of Management Journal*, 44(1): 95–105.

Coghlan, D. (2001) Insider Action Research Projects: Implication for Practicing Managers, *Management Learning*, 32(1): 49–60.

Coghlan, D. and Brannick, T. (2001) *Doing Action Research in your Own Organization.* Sage, London.

Cooperrider, D. L. and Srivastva, S. (1987) Appreciative Inquiry in Organizational Life, in W. Pasmore and R. Woodman (eds) *Research in Organizational Change and Development*, vol. 1. JAI, Greenwich, CT.

Cooperrider, D. and Whitney, D. (2001) A Positive Revolution in Change: Appreciative Inquiry, in D. L. Cooperrider, P. F. Sorensen, T. Yaeger and D. Whitney (eds) *Appreciative Inquiry: Rethinking Human Organization toward a Positive Theory of Change.* Stipes, Champaign, IL.

Cummings, T. and Worley, C. (2000) *Organization Development and Change*, 7th edition. South Western College Publishing, Cincinnati, OH.

Geisler, E. (1997) *Managing the Aftermath of Radical Corporate Change.* Quorum, Westport, CT.

Greenwood, D. and Levin, M. (1998) *Introduction to Action Research: Social Research for Social Change.* Sage, Thousand Oaks, CA.

Greiner, L. E. and Schein, V. E. (1988) *Power and Organization Development*. Addison-Wesley, Reading, MA.

Gummesson, E. (2000) *Qualitative Methods in Management Research*. Sage, Thousand Oaks, CA.

Janoff, S. and Weisbord, M. (2000) *Future Search*. Berrett-Koehler, San Francisco, CA.

Lawler, E., III (1985) Challenging Traditional Research Assumption, in E. Lawler, III, A. Mohrman, Jr, S. Mohrman, G. Ledford, T. Cummings and Associates (eds) *Doing Research that is Useful for Theory and Practice*. Lexington, Lanham, MD.

Lawler, E., III, Mohrman, A., Jr, Mohrman, S., Ledford, G., Cummings, T. and Associates (eds) (1985) *Doing Research that is Useful for Theory and Practice*. Lexington, Lanham, MD.

Lewin, K. (1973) Action Research and Minority Problems, in K. Lewin, *Resolving Social Conflicts: Selected Papers on Group Dynamics*, ed. G. Lewin. Souvenir Press, London.

Sharkey, L. and Sorensen, P. F. (2002) Survey Feedback: An Alternative to a Classic Intervention Experience in the U.S. Japan and India, *OD Practitioner*, 34(1): 43–46.

Sorensen, P., and Yaeger, T. (2003) Action Research as a Form of Data-Based Consulting. Paper presented at the Academy of Management Conference, Management Consulting Division, Seattle, Washington, August.

Sorensen, P., Yaeger, T., Keogh, D. and Bengtsson, U. (2003) Preliminary Findings on the International Application of Appreciative Inquiry as an Illustration of Integrating Local and Global Approaches to Management Research and Practice: A Three-Country Study. Paper presented at the European Academy of Management Conference, Milan, Italy.

Stensaker, I., Meyer, C., Falkenberg, J. and Haueng, A. (2001) Excessive Change: Unintended Consequences of Strategic Change. Best Paper Award presented at the Academy of Management Conference, Washington, DC.

Warrick, D. D. (2002) Organization Development: Past, Present and Future from the View of the Experts. Presented to the OD and Change Division Executive Committee, Academy of Management, Denver, CO.

Weisbord, M. (1987) *Productive Workplaces: Organizing and Managing for Dignity, Meaning, and Community*. Jossey-Bass, San Francisco, CA.

Whitney, D. and Trosten-Bloom, A. (2003) *The Power of Appreciative Inquiry: A Practical Guide to Positive Change*. Berrett-Koehler, San Francisco, CA.

Chapter 12

MBRR (Management by Research Results)

Pat Joynt

Context

During 1995 Henley Management College celebrated its fiftieth year of providing learning and development to managers and organizations. It was in that year that the International Centre for Management of Technology (ICMOT) was founded. The centre has the primary mission of Management by Research Results (MBRR) and has been closely connected to the new DBA programme at Henley. The centre is now represented by virtual associates from twenty countries. These include Australia, China, Brazil, Canada, Iceland, as well as the United Kingdom, United States, Norway, Sweden and Denmark.

In addition to the MBRR ongoing work with existing international DBA associates at Henley Management College, the centre has assisted in the sponsoring of leading Professors interested in reflecting on theory and research of doctoral associates who have used their own organizations for research and have reflected on the experience. The visiting professors at Henley have assisted in providing contributions to both understanding organization and to the development of the learning managers. These visiting professors included Professor Ed Schein from MIT in the United States, Professor Fred Luthans, former President of the Academy of Management and Professor Lavrids Hedaa, founder of the experience oriented MBA programme at the Copenhagen Business School.

Walking the talk

Several alternatives were evaluated when setting the reflective theme of this MBRR chapter. The main purpose is to integrate the MBRR theme with action research. Using a framework developed by Eden and Huxham (1996) offers us this opportunity. Drawing on the chapters of this book was one of the top alternatives. After closer scrutiny I felt that I did not have the necessary secondary data and background information to do this properly. The two exceptions to this were the chapters by Christopher Ibbott and Ann Parkinson, as their work was supervised by me at Henley Management

College. Another alternative was to use the works of Peter Nuttall and Peter Homa which were cited in Coghlan and Brannick (2001). A third alternative involved the nearly twenty action research theses that have been done at Henley.

In addition to the MBRR and action research criteria, I was interested in the key research concepts of generalizability and validity. The final sample takes all of the above criteria into consideration as well as a combination of the alternatives mentioned above. The sample for this chapter involves:

- The Ibbott and Parkinson works which are presented in Chapters 2 and 4.
- The Nuttall study of a large UK private organization and theses by Peter Homa and Helen Bevan (Bevan was added as her work complements Homa) on the United Kingdom National Health Service Change Programme, which has been called one of the largest change projects ever undertaken in a single organization.
- In attempting to generalize globally and across disciplines on the use of action research, I selected Les Bowd's work on top management strategy from Canada, the cross-cultural work of Betania Tanure de Barros in Brazil and the IT implementation thesis of Petter Gottschalk in Scandinavia.

It is worth noting that much of this action research has been carried further because five of the above sample are professors and directors of business schools. I have selected the abstracts from the theses in order to summarize work that varies from 200 to 800 pages. The general rule of thumb is that the abstract must tell the story in a page or two.

The National Health Service selected the Leicester Royal Infirmary as the hospital interested in making radical changes to health care. Helen Bevan and Peter Homa are now professors but still active in the NHS. Henley presently has three DBAs from the NHS studying for their doctorates in leadership of hospitals, implementation of change and decision making in the NHS.

Abstract from *Managing Today while Creating Tomorrow: Actionable Knowledge for Organisational Change in an NHS Hospital*

Helen Bevan – 1999

The study follows the temporal journey of a hospital's re-engineering programme programme over four years. The author, employed by the hospital as re-engineering programme leader, combines change practitioner, researcher and theory builder roles to create 'actionable knowledge'.

The nomothetic change approaches offered by many re-engineering methodologists were insufficient to guide the hospital change process. In addition to 'situational' process re-design, multifaceted changes were observed at leadership, internal community and individual levels. Rather than the anticipated model of change intervention creating desired organisational behaviour, contradictory and shifting factors within the hospital both shaped and were shaped by the progress of the change programme. Paradox emerged as a major theme. The hospital exhibited both an ambition for radical change ('creating tomorrow') and a need for significant stability ('managing today').

The re-engineering programme did not result in the expected patient process configuration. Rather a hybrid 'speciality process' model emerged. The adaptation of medical 'micro-power' was a significant factor. As a result, resources were reorganised around the patient's journey (process) through the hospital. However, patient groups were segmented by the nature of medical input (speciality) rather than by common patient need or flow rate (process). Whilst contradictions within the hybrid create tensions towards a process form, the strength of speciality and functional perspectives in the wider healthcare system suggest that a further hybrid is more likely than a future 'pure' process configuration.

Abstract from *Re-engineering the Leicester Royal Infirmary Healthcare Process*

Peter Homa – 1998

This study of the National Health Service's first whole hospital business process re-engineering programme provides a unique research opportunity. Further piquancy is added because the researcher is also the hospital's chief executive. This opens up a near ethnographic contextual examination of managing in the National Health Service at a time of tumultuous change. Operationalising the combined roles of chief executive and management researcher is one of this study's three contributions to management research. The research spans the period 1993–1996.

The hospital's early re-engineering programme results and consequential impact on the hospital's management structure and patient processes are described. A literature review culminates in a taxonomy of business process re-engineering writing and a synthesis of evidence based critical success factors. The research methodology uses a qualitative and quantitative approach through the medium of four revelatory case studies taken from The Leicester Royal Infirmary's re-engineering programme. Existing business process re-engineering theory is used to build the study's conceptual analytical framework and this generates four research questions and subsequent case study analysis. The case studies consider radical change attempted in four disparate areas of The Leicester Royal Infirmary. Attention is given to factors that contribute to the assessed motility of change evidenced in each case study. Comparative analysis of the four case studies distils analytical generalisations and enables development of as predictive model to help guide future healthcare re-engineering practitioners and researchers. The predictive model is the study's second contribution to management research. The predictive model distinguishes the intrinsic complexity of a healthcare process design from the difficulty of its implementation. The variables that contribute to the constructs of healthcare process complexity and healthcare process implementation difficulty are reviewed. The predictive model provides an analytical that develops a nomothetic approach in a highly context sensitive manner. Through this analytical prism, emergent management theory is propounded. This is the study's third contribution to management research.

The consonance and dissonance of this study's findings with extant business process re-engineering theory and practice is surveyed. The final chapter provides a reflexive account of the rites and responsibilities of the chief executive as management researcher.

Abstract from *Understanding 'Empowerment': A Study in a Manufacturing Company*

Peter Nuttall – 1998

Peter Nuttall was managing director of the company he used for his doctorate. He is now senior vice-president of the firm located in Paris.

This thesis continues the development of the complex management concept known as 'empowerment'. Using both quantitative and qualitative methods in a unique case study setting, the interactions at the core of the process of empowerment are exposed. Developing earlier research within a manufacturing environment, this research identifies many interacting phenomena, and real-life factors relating to the development of a business, within today's aggressively global scenario.

The role of head of the organisation is intertwined with that of researcher, to provide further insight into a unique combination in the field of management research. The access available to the case site, and the background understanding, offered a deeper penetration of the research; creating almost a longitudinal perspective, when compared with the more typically externally accessed research. The avoidance of bias and influence is dealt with comprehensively within this thesis.

The process of empowerment is broken down into three critical constructs: empowerment potential, empowerment opportunity and empowerment outcomes. The interaction of these three constructs is seen to be cyclical and a model of empowerment is developed which should form the basis for further research. The concluding chapter offers suggested implications for management policy in the future, and the linkage between empowerment and other motivational initiatives undertaken to stimulate improvement in order to survive, and grow a business within this competitive world.

Abstract from *Content Characteristics of Formal Information Technology Strategy as Implementation Predictors*

Petter Gottschalk – 1998

Prior to taking his doctorate, Petter Gottschalk had a top position in two leading Norwegian IT firms.

The need for improved implementation of information technology strategy has been emphasised in both empirical and prescriptive research studies. These studies show that implementation is important for four reasons. Firstly, the failure to carry out the IT strategy can cause lost opportunities, duplicated efforts, incompatible systems and wasted resources.

As well, the extent to which the IT strategy meets its objectives is determined by implementation. Further, the lack of implementation leaves firms dissatisfied with and reluctant to continue their strategic IT planning. Finally, the lack of implementation creates problems establishing and maintaining priorities in future strategic IT planning.

The main research question in this thesis is: 'What content characteristics of formal IT strategy predict the extent of plan implementation?' This research complements existing knowledge by addressing previous research from three sources: (i) empirical evaluation of the plan implementation link in the theory of strategic information systems planning; (ii) integration of research literature on organisational practices influencing the implementation; and (iii) application of validated instruments to measure potential predictors of the implementation. Ten content characteristics of formal information technology strategy were identified from the research literature as potential implementation predictors. These were descriptions of: (i) resources needed for the implementation; (ii) user involvement during the implementation; (iii) analyses of the organisation; (iv) anticipated changes in the external environment; (v) solutions to potential resistance during the implementation; (vi) information technology to be implemented; (vii) projects' relevance to the business plan; (viii) responsibility for the implementation; (ix) management support for the implementation; and (x) implementation issues clearly. Implementation hypotheses were then developed for the ten potential predictors.

The literature review in this thesis provides evidence that research and theory in the field of IT strategy implementation have moved beyond the early stages, making a sample survey appropriate to meet concerns about generalisation of results. The survey was conducted in Norway in 1997. The return of 471 completed questionnaires resulted in a satisfactory response rate of 43%. Formal IT strategy was reported in 40% of these organisations. Formal IT strategy was defined as 'a written plan comprised of projects for application of information technology to assist an organisation in realising its goals', while IT strategy implementation was defined as 'the process of completing the projects' The research results support the plan implementation link in the theory of strategic information systems planning. The two significant predictors in the testing of hypotheses are *description of responsibility for the implementation* and *description of user involvement during the implementation.* Based on the substantial amount of data collected, supplementary research results are presented, leading to potential modification of the theory. The thesis concludes with suggestions for further research.

Abstract from *Regional and Cross Cultural Differences and Similarities: Perception of Values of Brazilian Managers*

Betania Tanure de Barros – 2002

Betania Tanure de Barros is associated with one of the leading business schools in Brazil and is a frequent guest at INSEAD.

This study attempts to identify the perception of values of Brazilian managers stationed in four different regions of the country in terms of similarities and differences pertaining to these different regions regarding gender, age, type of organization (state-owned, privately-owned, domestic and multinational) and size. The research uses Geert Hofstede's instrument and theoretical construct: power distance, uncertainty avoidance, individualism versus collectivism, masculinity versus femininity and also long- versus short-term orientation. The purpose here is to identify and discuss differences and similarities between this study and that of Hofstede's original findings, which took place about three decades ago, using initially the first four dimensions and, by so doing, to test the validity of his theoretical construct.

Data was collected among executives from the 1,000 largest companies operating in Brazil (multinational corporations, privately-owned, domestic and state-owned organizations) as well as executives from other companies located in the four regions or states: São Paulo, Minas Gerais, Rio Grande do Sul and Ceará. The body of data included 895 valid questionnaire replies.

The review of the literature regarding issues about Brazil and cross-cultural management provided the basis for the formulation of the hypotheses and sub-hypotheses. The results found in the five dimensions were analyzed, discussed and compared to the previously formulated hypotheses, as well as with the scores which Hofstede found in his original four-dimension study and later for the fifth dimension that he included. Therefore, a longitudinal analysis was made in each of the dimensions: all of which were fully confirmed. Following the longitudinal analysis made for the general index the formulated sub-hypotheses were analyzed and discussed. Most sub-hypotheses were confirmed as well. In the cases of eventual deviations, they were fully discussed, what finally enabled the author to draw conclusions about the perception of values of Brazilian managers. Factor analysis was also discussed, including the main reasons for its applicability and implementation as well as the level of adequacy for its use in the present investigation. All data indicated the potential of individual factor analysis, despite Hofstede's emphasizing that his instrument would not be valid at the individual level, but at the ecological analysis level. The concepts of validity and reliability were also discussed proving the validity of the instrument used in the present study and its consequent reliability.

Finally, the author analyzed the implications of the research findings for management and indicated the possibilities for future research.

Abstract from *The Strategic Roles of Middle Managers, Collaborative Relationships between Top Management and the Middle, and the Impact of these Roles and Relationships on Organization Performance*

Les Bowd – 2003

Since 1980, two areas have dominated research into the strategic management process. First, is the large body of work focusing on the role of the top management team (TMT) in the strategic process. Much of this research has its roots in Hambrick and Mason's [1984] upper echelons theory. Strategic decision-making (SDM) is the second element of the strategic process where researchers have concentrated their efforts, pursuing issues of content, context and process. While researchers generally sought out those factors that contributed to SDM effectiveness, there has been a tendency to focus attention on how the TMT makes strategic decisions. Although improved organization performance has been attributed to characteristics of the TMT and SDM process, relatively little research existed prior to 1990 on how strategy was implemented effectively. More significantly, minimal attention was paid to those being asked to lead the implementation, the middle manager.

Ironically, it was in the wake of dramatic downsizing and re-engineering, in the early 1990s, that both practitioners and academic researchers began to recognize the significance and strategic impact of 'the middle' on many phases of the strategic management process.

This research investigates the roles and relationships of middle managers in the strategic process and the impact they have on organization performance. A comprehensive review of relevant literature, including that which addresses strategic decision making, strategy implementation, top management team and middle management strategic behaviour, was used to establish the strategic significance of middle managers and act as a foundation for the research. Replication of the work of [Steven] Floyd and [William] Wooldridge was undertaken to confirm the strategic roles fulfilled by middle managers in the formulation and implementation of organization strategy. If, and how, these strategic roles, and the influence that accompanies them, impacted organization performance was another focus of this research. How the strategic roles of the TMT and middle managers interact, to shape and implement strategy, was investigated by attempting to replicate the work of [Stuart] Hart and [Catherine] Banbury. The replicated model formed the basis of an investigation of the impact of strategy making modes on organization performance. Utilizing constructs developed by Miller (1997) implementation effectiveness was assessed and its relationship with organization performance evaluated. Lastly, efforts were made to identify possible interrelationships between middle management strategic roles, organization strategy making modes and organization performance.

Data representing the responses of 132 managers, predominantly at middle levels, in 40 organizations, replicated the strategic roles model outlined by Floyd and Wooldridge. This gave strong support to the validity and generalizability of the concept that postulated four key strategic roles. Championing alternatives and synthesizing information that provide upward influence, and facilitating adaptability and implementing deliberate strategy, which provide downward influence. Correlations and regression analysis demonstrated a moderate relationship between the strategic roles and organization performance. This was consistent with the original research and suggests a complex relationship between strategic roles, influence and performance. Perceived upward influence was marginally greater than downward, but downward influence appears to more directly effect performance. However, this was a moderate to weak relationship.

The same sample casts some doubt on the generalizability of the Hart and Banbury strategy modes model. However, although it was not possible to fully replicate the model produced from their research, the findings of this work do support the conceptual orientation of their model and proposes a model that has three of five modes in common, with two others sharing similar characteristics. It appears that situational factors, including structure of the questionnaire, the managerial group sampled, and the industry and business environment of the respondents may impact responses. However, in the conceptual model tested by this researcher, all strategy modes featuring collaboration between top management and others, including the middle had a very strong relationship with performance variables, and the cumulative model shows three of the modes combining for a strong impact on performance.

MBRR reflections

I have had experience as an executive officer in the Navy and as a power company manager and executive. I began my doctorate with all this experience behind me and often found the that road was not easy because of the heavy emphasis on theoretical and not experiential contributions.

Thanks to the examples above and the ICMOT orientation towards Management by Research Results, the world is changing both academically and practically.

Our framework for the analysis of the work presented through abstracts will come from the action research area, which has a rich tradition of conceptual insights (Lewin, 1948; Revans, 1982; Argyris, 1991; Argyris and Schön, 1978; Denzin and Lincoln, 1994; Emery and Thorsrud, 1969). It is beyond the scope of this chapter to define action research in detail; however, I would like to use the framework developed by Eden and Huxham (1996) to summarize our reflections on the abstracts presented. Eden and Huxham used fifteen characteristics to define action research in an organizational context. Each characteristic will be presented followed by my reflections.

Action research characteristic 1

Action research demands an integral involvement by the researcher in an intent to change the organization. This intent may not succeed – no change may take place as a result of the intervention – and the change may not be as intended.

Reflection

Bevan, who was the project leader in a large NHS radical change financed by the United Kingdom government, and Homa, who was the head of the hospital involved, are probably the best examples of this integration. Ibbott is also a good example. Due to the short term of observation in most doctoral work, the main goal is often understanding and describing the present reality rather than changing it. But I would argue that a deeper understanding often leads to intended and/or unintended changes. This has been the case with the work being reviewed here.

I quote from recent correspondence from Professor Homa, one of the two cases from the Leicester Hospital.

> In Leicester we learnt more from our mistakes and the DBA programme helped to provide an analytic prism through which good and bad experience was refracted to extract actionable knowledge as to how to do better next time. This type of knowledge has application both in the setting in which it is generated but also in subsequent settings where change is attempted. The change practitioners in effect become more expert (one hopes!) and therefore more able to bring about successful change.

Action research characteristic 2

Action research must have some implications beyond those required for action or generation of knowledge in the domain of the project. It must be possible to envisage talking about the theories developed in relation to other situations. Thus it must be clear that the results could inform other contexts, at least in the sense of suggesting areas for consideration.

Reflection

This was one of the strongest characteristics found in all the work presented. Part of a doctorate degree usually involves a final chapter that asks how other contexts can be informed and what improvements can be made in future work. As an example Bevan's work has been used to help develop national policy in the United Kingdom. This includes the way in which the adoption of the classic improvement methods (suitably customized for healthcare) and their diffusion across the NHS.

Action research characteristic 3

As well as being usable in everyday life, action research demands valuing theory, with theory elaboration and development as an explicit concern of the research process. This is one of the essential ingredients in DBA work.

Reflection

Valuing theory is the essence of doctorate work. All of the theses have a comprehensive literature review chapter with a follow-up in the conclusions.

Action research characteristic 4

If the generality drawn out of the action research is to be expressed through the design of tools, techniques, models and method then this, alone, is not enough; the basis for their design must be explicit and shown to be related to the theories with inform the design and which, in turn, are supported or developed through action research.

Reflection

Tools and techniques are not the essence of research but models and methods are. The research questions represented here were derived from related theories and then tested for their application in the real world.

Action research characteristic 5

Action research will be concerned with a system of emergent theory, in which the theory develops from a synthesis of that which emerges from the use in practice of the body of theory which informed the intervention and research intent.

Reflection

Whenever theory is tested in real life, the emergent results result in contributions to the theories being tested, thus a synthesis emerges.

Action research characteristic 6

Theory building, as a result of action research, will be incremental, moving through a cycle of developing theory-to-reflection-to-developing theory from the particular to the general in small steps.

Reflection

The metaphor often used in the research reported is a 'grain of sand' being placed on the mountain of theory. In addition reflection of results becomes a critical issue.

Action research characteristic 7

What is important for action research is not a (false) dichotomy between prescription and description, but a recognition that description will be prescription, even if implicitly so. Thus presenters of action research should be clear about what they expect the consumer to take from it and present it with a form and style appropriate to this aim.

Reflection

Most doctorate work is done with negative hypothesis testing. The emphasis is on observation and description not prescription although this may occur in generalities. As an interesting point, the Leicester Hospital change work was reported in video style with the aim of presenting it to prospective consumers.

Action research characteristic 8

For good quality action research a high degree of systematic method and orderliness is required in reflecting about and holding on to, the research data and the emergent theoretical outcomes of each episode or cycle of involvement in the organization.

Reflection

This is the essence of doctorate method:

> introduction → context → literature review
> → analyses → conclusions.

Action research characteristic 9

For action research, the processes of exploration of the data – rather than collection of the data – in the detecting of emergent theories and development of existing theories, must either be replicable or, at least, capable of being explained to others.

Reflection

Replicability is an essential criterion in doctorate work.

Action research characteristic 10

Adhering to the nine characteristics above is a necessary but not sufficient condition for the validity of action research.

Reflection

Table 12.1 reflects the summary of the theses mentioned earlier as well as Ibbott's and Parkinson's chapters in this book.

Action research characteristic 11

The full process of action research involves a series of interconnected cycles, where writing about research outcomes at the latter stages of an action

Table 12.1 Doctorate thesis: action research characteristics

Action research characteristic	Bevan	Homa	Nuttall	Gottschalk	de Barros	Bowd	Ibbott	Parkinson
1 Integral involvement	X	X	X	X	X	X	X	X
2 Results inform other contexts	X	X	X	X	X	X	X	X
3 Theory elaboration	X	X	X	X	X	X	X	X
4 Explicit design	X	X	X	X	X	X	X	X
5 Concerned with emergent theory	X	X	X	X	X	X	X	X
6 Incremental theory building	X	X	X	X	X	X	X	X
7 Descriptive	X	X	X	X	X	X	X	X
8 Systematic method	–	X	X	X	X	X	X	–
9 Replicable	–	X	X	X	X	X	X	–

Note
X, complied; –, marginal compliance.

research project is an important aspect of theory exploration and development, combining the processes of explicating pre-understanding and methodical reflection to explore and develop theory formally.

Reflection

All doctors are encouraged to continue with their work. In fact most theses have a section on 'suggestions for future research'. Using the sample of eight from Table 12.1, only one or two have not pursued the strategy of further research in the area in which they were interested. I estimate that six of the eight have done major work in the action research area after receiving their doctorate.

Action research characteristic 12

It is difficult to justify the use of action research when the same aims can be satisfied using approaches (such as controlled experimentation or surveys) that can demonstrate the link between data and outcomes more transparently. Thus in action research, the reflection and data collection process – and hence the emergent theories – are most valuably focused on the aspects that cannot be captured by other approaches.

Reflection

This was the most difficult characteristic from Eden and Huxham (1966) to evaluate. Most theses involve multiple methods even if they only occur in the pilot test stage. One could argue that the ongoing quest for knowledge results in any doctorate work being debated and revised or duplicated possibly using other methodologies.

Action research characteristic 13

In action research, the opportunities for triangulation that do not offer themselves with other methods should be exploited fully and reported. They should be used as a dialectical device which powerfully facilitates the incremental development of theory.

Reflection

This characteristic is one of the strongest in the research summarized here. The dialectical nature of pilot tests and combining questionnaire results with follow-up interviews cannot be underestimated. The whole process could be labelled incremental development.

Action research characteristic 14

The history and context for the intervention must be taken as critical to the interpretation of the likely range of validity and applicability of the results of action research.

Reflection

There are two points to make here. First, context is often an essential part of qualitative research; often it deserves a separate chapter. The second point involves validity and applicability. The very nature of the research process, which involves enough information for duplication, aides in making the results valid and applicable over time.

Action research characteristic 15

Action research requires that the theory development which is of general value is disseminated in such a way as to be of interest to an audience wider than those integrally involved with the action and/or with the research.

Reflection

Dissemination of action-oriented research at the doctoral level should be a high priority, but most practitioners avoid reading the highly technical literature review and methodology chapters. Perhaps the best strategy is to emphasize the dissemination of the first and the last chapters which often have an easier journalistic approach. A review of the eight theses reported here shows that much could be learned from just reading the last chapter.

Conclusion

Let us return to the comments from Professor Peter Homa on an earlier draft:

> Organizations only transform if their citizens (staff) are supported to transform their capacity to bring about change. This might be viewed as the move of staff from organizational subjects, to citizens, to leaders. The HMC experience, at least through the DBA, encourages participants to recognize this and how it may be accomplished.
>
> The average DBA research associate brings a good deal of management experience and this enriches their capacity to 'make sense' of the utility of management modes or theories. It helps to confound the observation that we live forward but understand backwards.
>
> A personal view of mine is that leaders can't lead others until they can lead themselves. The DBA type experience encourages participants to understand themselves more skillfully. Hopefully, as managers this means that their enterprises benefit from more competent stewardship and performance.

References

Argyris, C. (1991) Teaching Smart People How to Learn, *Harvard Business Review*, May–June: 99–109.

Argyris, C. and Schön, D. A. (1978) *Organizational Learning: A Theory of Action Perspective*. Addison-Wesley, Reading, MA.

Coghlan, D. and Brannick, T. (2001) *Doing Action Research in your Own Organization*. Sage, London.

Denzin, N. and Lincoln, N. (eds) (1994) *Handbook of Qualitative Research*. Sage, London.

Eden, C. and Huxham, C. (1966) Action Research for the Study of Organizations, in S. Clegg, C. Hardy and W. Nord (eds) *Handbook of Organization Studies*. Sage, Beverly Hills, CA.

Emery, F. and Thorsrud, E. (1969) *Democracy at Work*. Martinus Nyhoff, Leiden.

Hambrick, D. C. and Mason, P. A. (1984) Upper Echelons: The Organization as a Reflection of its Top Managers, *Academy of Management Review*, 9: 193–206.

Lewin, K. (1948) *Resolving Social Conflicts*. HarperCollins, New York.

Miller, S. (1997) Implementing Strategic Decisions: Four Key Success Factors, *Organization Studies*, 18(4): 577–602.

Revans, R. W. (1982) *The Origins and Growth of Action Learning*. Chartwell Bratt, Brickley, UK.

Chapter 13

Managers as learners and researchers

David Coghlan

Our subject in this book has been to explore the question of whether the learning-in-action of individual managers can contribute, not only to their own learning and that of their organizations, but also to our knowledge of organizations, and help to generate theory about what organizations are really like and how they work. In other words, can managers who learn-in-action be researchers at the same time? We have formulated our answer around the experience of nine managers who, through participation in postgraduate programmes which cater for the practising manager, have engaged in research-in-action in their respective organizations.

Managers as learners

How do managers learn? Coghlan and Brannick (2001) present four activities: experiencing, reflecting, interpreting and taking action.

- *Experiencing*: as managers go through their daily work life they experience a great deal. Some of their experiences are planned, others unplanned. Some are what is done to them by others. Some experiences are cognitive; they occur through the intellectual processes of thinking and understanding. Some occur in feelings and emotions. At times managers may feel excited, angry, frustrated, sad, lonely and so on. Other experiences may be experienced in the body – excited energy, embarrassed blushing, tightness in the stomach, headaches, ulcers or sickness. These three domains – cognitive, feelings and body awareness – are where experiencing occurs and managers can learn by attending to these.
- *Reflecting*: attending to experience is the first step to learning. The second step is to stand back from these experiences and inquire into them. In action learning, questioning programmed knowledge is the key to learning (Pedler, 1996). Managers may ask themselves, what is it that I do not yet understand? What is it that has me feeling angry?
- *Interpreting*: interpreting is where they find answers to the questions

posed in the reflection. They draw on theories and constructs to help them make sense of their experience.

- *Taking action:* what do managers do as a result of their reflecting and interpreting? It may be that they decide to behave differently the next time they are in a similar situation in order not to repeat the previous experience or in order to create a different outcome.

These four activities operate as a cycle where experiencing, reflecting, interpreting and taking action set up another cycle of experiencing and so on. Learning becomes a continuous cycle through life. Learning is not any one of these four activities on its own but each of them together. Managers need to develop skills at each activity: be able to experience directly, be able to stand back and ask questions, be able to conceptualize answers to their questions, and be able to take risks and experiment in similar or new situations.

They may of course block learning at each activity. They may view experiencing as predictable, routine and uninvolving from which they are detached. They may see reflecting as a luxury, an activity for which they do not have any time. They may disregard the conceptualization which accompanies interpreting as something for academics and apart from the 'real world'. They may not engage in taking new action because of a fear of taking risks or of rocking the boat. These are ways in which managers, or indeed any individual, may close themselves to learning.

Reflection

Reflection is the process of stepping back from experience to process what the experience means, with a view to planning further action. It is the critical link between the concrete experience, the interpretation and taking new action. As Raelin (2000) discusses, it is the key to learning as it enables managers to develop the ability to uncover and make explicit to themselves what they have planned, discovered and achieved in practice. He also argues that reflection must be brought into the open so that it goes beyond privately held taken-for-granted assumptions and helps managers to see how their knowledge is constructed.

Mezirow (1991) identifies three forms of reflection – content, process and premise. These are useful categories. *Content* reflection is where managers think about the issues, what is happening, etc. *Process* reflection is where they think about strategies, procedures and how things are being done. *Premise* reflection is where they critique underlying assumptions and perspectives. All three forms of reflection are critical. Christopher Ibbott stands back from his experience of managing *eRelationship* and explicitly identifies the premises underpinning the transformational change.

The managers in their respective chapters have shown how they took their experience to reflection. They have drawn on organizational and managerial frameworks to help them reflect on what was happening around them and those frameworks provide the basis for planning subsequent action. Derek Whelan's use of Gabarro's framework for the new manager enabled him to make sense of the stages he was going through in taking over the family business.

Managers as researchers

When we think of research, we typically think of two features. The first is that research is concerned with producing knowledge and developing theory. The second is that research primarily addresses the audience of the community of scholars. In contrast, we, in this book, are promoting a form of research, called action research, which aims to integrate both theory and action and which engages in three strategies, first, second and third person research and practice (Reason, 2001).

The primary purpose of action research is to produce practical knowledge which is embodied in daily actions by the manager-researcher and the development of learning organizations and which aims to guide inquiry and action in the present. Action research is collaborative in that it aims to enhance people's involvement in the generation of knowledge about them and their work and the actions they take. This is in keeping with the general understanding of the processes of organizational learning. Action research is rooted in each participant's experience of the situation, rather than being removed from it. Finally, action research is not grounded in formal propositions but is a human activity which draws on different forms of knowing.

With respect to the three strategies of research,

- *First person* research addresses the ability of managers to develop an inquiring approach to their own life by becoming aware of their own thought processes, feelings, assumptions and values, and how they affect choices and actions. Akinyinka Akinyele begins from first person and grounds his own personal values in his family upbringing. He then shows how he works to bring these values to bear on his second person engagement with his staff.
- *Second person* research addresses the ability of managers to inquire with others into issues of mutual concern and create communities of inquiry in the communities of practice which are managers' teams, groups and organizational colleagues.
- *Third person* research aims at creating a community of inquiry which is broader than those directly involved in the research, and has an impersonal quality to it.

Cynthia Deane explicitly integrates all three persons in her chapter. As she describes the interventions she initiated with her staff aimed at enabling organizational learning (second person practice) and reflects on her own personal learning (first person) and on what other organizations might take from the experience of her organization (third person).

The dynamics of managers learning in and researching their own organizations

Action research is generally framed with the action researcher as the 'friendly outsider', that is, one who facilitates learning and change in the manner of an external organization development consultant. Action research by insiders has its own dynamics which distinguish it from an external action researcher approach (Coghlan, 2001; Coghlan and Brannick, 2001). The researchers are already immersed in the organization and have a pre-understanding from being an actor in the processes being studied and have a political stake in the organization for their careers.

There are a number of significant challenges for those managers who undertake action research in their own organization which I will explore under the following headings: pre-understanding, role duality and organizational politics.

Pre-understanding

Pre-understanding refers to such things as people's knowledge, insights and experience before they engage in an action research programme. The knowledge, insights and experience of the manager action researchers apply, not only to theoretical understanding of organizational dynamics, but also to the lived experience of their own organization. The key challenge is to hold both closeness to the data and have distance from it.

Role duality

When manager action researchers augment their normal organizational membership roles with the research enterprise, they are likely to encounter role conflict and find themselves caught between loyalty tugs, behavioural claims and identification dilemmas.

Managing organizational politics

Undertaking an action research project in one's own organization is political and might even be considered subversive. This is because action research examines everything, stresses listening, emphasizes questioning, fosters courage, incites action, abets reflection and endorses democratic participation. Any or all of these characteristics may be threatening to existing organizational norms. Accordingly, manager action researchers need to be politically astute in deciding to engage in action research. They need to be prepared to work the political system, which involves balancing the organization's formal justification of what it wants in the project with their own tacit personal justification for political activity. Throughout the project they have to maintain their credibility as an effective driver of change and as an astute political player. The key to this is assessing the power and interests of relevant stakeholders in relation to aspects of the project. Paddy McDermott reflects on the politics of managing a subsidiary of a multinational and shows how difficult it is to balance the agendas of the head office and the subsidiary. On the individual level, Thomas Schmidt reflects on the political activity of 'backstaging' and notes that he learned that it is important to be true to oneself.

Contributing to organizational knowledge and learning

The question then arises, how do the action research projects of individual managers contribute to both the ongoing learning of the organizations in which these manager-researchers work and to the community of organizational scholars? The integration of first and second person research and individual and organizational learning occurs through attention to the levels of aggregation that exist in organizations. These levels describe, not only levels of analysis such as individual, team, interdepartmental group and organization, but also interlevel dynamics such as the impact the individual has on the team and vice versa, the team on other teams, and the organization on individuals, teams and the interdepartmental group and vice versa (Rashford and Coghlan, 1994; Coghlan, 2002). Such interlevel dynamics are integral to the nature of organizations as recursive systems and attention to them is critical to the processes of organizational change and learning.

First, there is the first person individual learning and change level for manager-researchers, whereby they attend to their own learning-in-action through their managerial actions. Akinyele's, Whelan's and Deane's chapters contain examples of such personal learning. Yet individual manager-researchers' own personal learning and change is not sufficient if they aim to effect change in larger and more complex systems than themselves. Typically, the most immediate experience individuals have of an organization is as a member of a team or group. It is through that membership that individuals exercise their role and influence. Hence, the second level of attention is to the dynamics of the teams in which they work and utilize in their projects. Such attention involves attending to content, process and premise issues. For a team to learn, its members need to attend and engage in dialogue on such issues as how its members communicate among themselves, solve problems, make decisions and so on.

Yet the research and change process cannot be restricted to learning and change by individuals and teams alone. The learning and change which take place in individuals and teams need to be generalized across the inter-departmental group, whereby other teams and units engage in dialogue and negotiation. A critical focus for attention in this regard is the impacts that cultural perspectives from different functions have on the change process. Intergroup dialogue needs to take account of how functional areas in organizations hold different assumptions from and about one another.

Finally, the research project does not stop within the organization. Organizations as open systems have a dynamic two-way relationship with their external environment. The research process needs to include how the organization is affecting, and being affected by, its customers or clients, stakeholders, local community, competitors, wider society and other organizations. Ibbott's and McDermott's chapters are accounts of inter-organizational dynamics, one in supply chain management, the other in corporate–subsidiary relations.

Viewing organizations through levels of analysis is only one part of the picture. The other part refers to how each of the levels is related to each of the others (Coghlan, 2002). There is an essential interlevel element in that each level has a dynamic relationship with each of the others. This relationship is grounded in systems dynamics, whereby the relationship each of the four levels has with the other three is systemic, with feedback loops forming a complex pattern of relationships. Dysfunctions at any of the four levels can cause dysfunctions at any of the other three levels. An individual's level of disaffection may be expressed in dysfunctional behaviour in the team and affect a team's ability to function effectively, which in turn reinforces the individual's disaffection. If a team is not functioning effectively, it can limit the interdepartmental group's effectiveness, which may depend on the quality and timeliness of information, resources and partially completed work from that team. If the interdepartmental group's multiple activities are not co-ordinated, the organization's ability to compete effectively may be affected. In systemic terms, each of the four levels affects each of the other three.

For manager action researchers, the political dynamics of framing and selecting an action research project, of using their pre-understanding and the action research process to assess the scope of the issue and the degree of political support and/or opposition involve working with individuals, teams, across the interdepartmental group in order that individual learning can be aggregated into organizational learning. Such dynamics are critical to bridge the wide gap which exists between individual and organizational learning.

- It is an engagement in *first person* research/skills for managers who attempt to learn-in-action and develop an inquiring approach to their own life, act purposefully and learn from experience.
- It is an engagement in *second person* research/skills in fostering face-to-face work with others in inquiring into organizational issues, developing

strategies, implementing plans and evaluating outcomes, and so building learning in organizations.

● It is an engagement in *third person* research/skills through disseminating usable theory and contributing valuable knowledge as to what it is really like in organizations.

Conclusion

In this chapter I have reflected on managers as learners-in-action and as action researchers. Learning-in-action involves attending to experience through reflecting and interpreting experience and then taking action. Action research works through a similar process with the process of inquiry going beyond subjective learning to an integration of first, second and third person research and practice. It aims to contribute to the more effective functioning of organizational systems and to contribute to science.

Each of the managers who have contributed to this volume has engaged in researching in his or her own organization and has enacted the role of the practitioner-researcher, as Jarvis (1999) expresses it, or the scholar-practitioner as Peter Sorensen has discussed in his chapter. The academic programmes in which each participated are constructed to meet the exigencies of the practising manager engaged in learning and research in action. Their example, we hope, adds not only to the literature on management learning, research and education but also to the literature on the management of change through the specific issues each respective manager confronted.

References

Coghlan, D. (2001) Insider Action Research Projects: Implications for Practising Managers, *Management Learning*, 32(1): 49–60.

Coghlan, D. (2002) Interlevel Dynamics in Systemic Action Research, *Systemic Practice and Action Research*, 15(4): 273–283.

Coghlan, D. and Brannick, T. (2001) *Doing Action Research in your Own Organization*. Sage, London.

Jarvis, P. (1999) *The Practitioner-Researcher*. Jossey-Bass, San Francisco, CA.

Mezirow, J. (1991) *Transformative Dimensions of Adult Learning*. Jossey-Bass, San Francisco, CA.

Pedler, M. (1996) *Action Learning for Managers*. Lemos and Crane, London.

Raelin, J. (2000) *Work-Based Learning: The New Frontier of Management Development*. Prentice Hall, Upper Saddle River, NJ.

Rashford, N. S. and Coghlan, D. (1994) *The Dynamics of Organizational Levels: A Change Framework for Managers and Consultants*. Addison-Wesley, Reading, MA.

Reason, P. (2001) Learning and Change through Action Research, in J. Henry (ed.) *Creative Management*, 2nd edition. Sage, London.

Index